Jurisdictional Competition

Europa Law Publishing, Groningen 2009

Jurisdictional Competition

Selected Cases in International and European Law

Dr. Nikolaos Lavranos

Europa Law Publishing is a publishing company specializing in European Union law, international trade law, public international law, environmental law and comparative national law.
For further information please contact Europa Law Publishing via email: info@europalawpublishing.com or visit our website at: www.europalawpublishing.com.

Typeset in Scala and Scala Sans, Graphic design by G2K Designers, Groningen/Amsterdam

NUR 828; ISBN 978-90-8952-067-8

Mixed Sources
Productgroep uit goed beheerde bossen, gecontroleerde bronnen en gerecycled materiaal.
www.fsc.org Cert no. CU-COC-803615
© 1996 Forest Stewardship Council
FSC

Acknowledgments

This book represents the final outcome of the research project entitled 'Competing Jurisdictions between the ECJ and other international courts and tribunals' that has been generously funded by the Netherlands Organisation for Scientific Research (NWO). The research started in January 2005 and originally was supposed to last for 3 years. But due to the fact that I partly left academia the project was extended until March 2009. This book was concluded in the context of a Max Weber Fellowship that was awarded for the academic year 2008/09 by the European University Institute (EUI), Florence.

In the course of pursuing this research project, the author has had the privilege to engage in many stimulating discussions with many very kind and critical colleagues around the world – too many to acknowledge them all individually.

However, the author is in particular grateful to Prof. André Nollkaemper, Director of the Amsterdam Centre of International Law (ACIL) who initiated my thinking on this topic and supported the grant application. Prof. Ernst Ulrich Petersmann, Head of the Law Department of the European University Institute (EUI) in Florence deserves very special acknowledgements for inviting me as a Max Weber Fellow to the EUI and for the very simulating cooperation between us.

Very special thanks are also due to my colleagues at Hebrew University, in particular, Prof. Yuval Shany, Dr. Tomer Broude, Dr. Guy Harpaz and Dr. Iris Canor who over time have become dear friends. Special thanks are also due to Dr. Giuseppe Martinico of the Sant'Anna School of Advance Studies in Pisa.

I am also indebted to the creators of the Project on International Courts and Tribunals (PICT), Prof. Cesare Romano, Dr. Ruth Mackenzie and Prof. Philippe Sands.

Finally, I wish to thank my former assistant Nick Vielliard for his excellent assistance during his one-year LLM-stint at the University of Amsterdam, Law Faculty.

Above all, however, this book is dedicated to the infinite love and support of my wife Simone and my son Luca.

N. Lavranos

Abbreviations

AJIL	American Journal of International Law
Am.U. Int'l L.Rev.	American University International Law Review
ASIL Proc.	American Society of International Law Proceedings
Asper Rev.Int'l B.&T.L.	Asper Review of International Business and Trade Law
B.C.Int'l&Comp.L.Rev.	Boston College International and Comparative Law Review
CDE	Cahiers de Droit Européen
Ch.J.Int'l L.	Chicago Journal of International Law
CML Rev.	Common Market Law Review
Col. J. Transnat'l L.	Columbia Journal of Transnational Law
EConLRev.	European Constitutional Law Review
EEEL Rev.	European Energy and Environmental Law Review
EEL Rev.	European Environmental Law Review
EFA Rev.	European Foreign Affairs Review
EJIL	European Journal of International Law
EJLS	European Journal of Legal Studies
EL Rep.	European Law Reporter
EL Rev.	European Law Review
EPL	European Public Law
EuGRZ	Europäische Grundrechte Zeitschrift
EuR	Europarecht
Fordham Int'l L. J.	Fordham International Law Journal
GLJ	German Law Journal
Harv. Int'l L. J.	Harvard International Law Journal
HRLRev.	Human Rights Law Review
HYbIL	Hague Yearbook of International Law
ICLQ	International and Comparative Law Quarterly
Int'l T.L.&Reg.	International Trade Law and Regulation
Iowa L. Rev.	Iowa Law Review
J. Int'l Arb.	Journal of International Arbitration
J. Int'l Comm.&Econ.	Journal of International Commerce and Economics
J. Int'l L.&Int'l Rel.	Journal of International Law and International Relations
JDI	Journal du Droit International
JEL	Journal of Environmental Law
JICJ	Journal of International Criminal Justice
JIEL	Journal of International Economic Law
JWT	Journal of World Trade
KJ	Kritische Justiz
L&PICT	Law and Practice of International Courts and Tribunals
LIEI	Legal Issues of Economic Integration
LJIL	Leiden Journal of International Law
Mich. J. Int'l L.	Michigan Journal of International Law
Minn. J. Int'l L.	Minnesota Journal of International Law

Minn. J.Gl.T.	Minnesota Journal of Global Trade
MPYbUN L.	Max Planck Yearbook of UN Law
N.C.J.Int'l L.&C.Reg.	North Carolina Journal of International Law & Commercial Regulation
NJIL	Nordic Journal of International Law
NJW	Neue Juristische Wochenschrift
NYU J. Int'l L&Pol.	New York University Journal of International Law and Politics
Rev.B.D.I.	Revue Belge du Droit International
Rev.trim.D.Eur.	Revue trimestrielle de Droit Européen
Stan.L.Rev.	Stanford Law Review
Tex.Hisp. J.L.&Pol.	Texas Hispanic Journal of Law and Policy
Tex.Int'l L.J.	Texas International Law Journal
Uni.Ill. L.Rev.	University of Illinois Law Review
Va. J. Int'l L.	Virginia Journal of International Law
WT Rev.	World Trade Review
Yale J. Int'l L.	Yale Journal of International Law
ZEuS	Zeitschrift für Europarechtliche Studien

CHAPTER I

Introduction

The issue of competing jurisdictions is certainly not new to law. It has long been known in domestic law, for instance regarding the delineation of jurisdiction between civil and administrative courts[1], between federal and state/local courts[2] and between ordinary courts and constitutional courts[3]. Similarly, issues of competing jurisdictions have been dealt with many times in private international law cases in which domestic courts of different nations have to determine whether they or a foreign court have jurisdiction to adjudicate a certain case.[4] Equally, in many foreign investment cases the question has to be answered of which court or tribunal has jurisdiction to decide, or whether a court or tribunal should exercise its jurisdiction if another court has already issued a decision regarding the same dispute.[5]

However, for public international law the issue of competing jurisdictions is relatively new. For example, in 1999 the ICTY kicked off the jurisdictional debate when it explicitly deviated from the ICJ's *Nicaragua test* regarding the conditions to be met for state and subsequently individual responsibility.[6] Whereas the ICTY considered itself competent to determine the conditions for individual responsibility, which also necessitated a determination of the conditions for state responsibility[7], the ICJ in its *Genocide Convention* judgment[8] of 2007 flatly rejected the claim of competence by the ICTY.

As regards European Community law, the debate on jurisdictional competition has focused primarily on the *vertical relationship* between the domestic courts of the EC Member States vis-à-vis the European Court of Justice (ECJ). A well-known example is the still continuing struggle between the German Federal Constitutional Court (hereinafter Bundesverfassungsgericht, BVerfG) and the ECJ on the exact delineation of their respective jurisdictional competence. Similar, though maybe less politicized, struggles over jurisdictional delineation have also taken place between the French and Italian supreme and constitutional courts and the ECJ.[9]

In order to deal with its jurisdictional competition with the ECJ, the BVerfG has developed and adopted the *Solange* method, which allows it to accept or reject the exclusive jurisdictional authority of the ECJ on a flexible basis. In

1 In France a special court, the *Tribunal des Conflits*, has even been created to decide on jurisdictional conflicts between the civil and administrative courts.

2 This problem arises in most, if not all, federal systems, such as the US and Germany.

3 This issue arises in most, if not all, states that have a constitutional court as the highest judicial body next to the ordinary courts. Germany is again a good example.

4 See e.g.: Cheshire / North / Fawcett (2008).

5 See e.g.: McLachlan / Shore / Weiniger (2007).

6 See the following contributions: Kreß (2007); Gaeta (2007); Cassese (2007); Milanovic (2007); Gattini (2007a).

7 See e.g.: ICTY Appeals Chamber *Tadic*, judgment of 15 July 1999.

8 ICJ *Genocide Convention Application of the Convention on the Prevention and Punishment of the Crime of Genocide* (Bosnia Herzegovina v Serbia and Montenegro), judgment of 26.2.2007.

9 Craig (2002).

short, as long as the BVerfG considers the fundamental rights protection offered by the ECJ to be comparable to its own, the BVerfG will – in principle – not exercise its jurisdiction.[10] It suffices to mention here that the struggle continues, as was indicated for instance by the BVerfG's *European Arrest Warrant* judgment[11], and more recently by the attack on the ECJ by the former President of the BVerfG and former German President Roman Herzog.[12]

However, this book is not concerned with the *vertical* jurisdictional *relationship* between national and European courts, but rather with *horizontal jurisdictional competition* between the ECJ and other international courts, as well as between international courts and tribunals in general.

Until recently, the main issue of *horizontal jurisdictional competition* involving the ECJ was that concerning its relationship with the European Court of Human Rights (ECrtHR).[13] Ever since the ECJ started integrating and applying the European Convention on Human Rights (ECHR) into the Community legal order, the question has become acute of whether this undermines the jurisdiction of the ECrtHR, which is the principle court for determining the fundamental rights standard within the context of the ECHR. While an active judicial dialogue between the ECJ and the ECrtHR has been taking place for at least two decades now[14], the delineation of their respective jurisdiction was only recently explicitly addressed, and to some extent clarified, by the ECrtHR's *Bosphorus* judgment.[15] In that judgment the ECrtHR stated that it considered the level of fundamental rights protection within the EC comparable to that of the ECHR, so that – in principle – it would not review the compatibility of measures adopted by Member States for the purpose of implementing EC law obligations under the ECHR, unless the fundamental rights protection offered by the ECJ were 'manifestly deficient'.[16] This is essentially an application of the BVerfG's *Solange* method.[17]

More recently, however, the issue of *horizontal jurisdictional competition* involving the ECJ has also emerged in regard to other international courts and (arbitral) tribunals. For example, in the context of the *MOX plant* dispute between Ireland and the UK, the issue arose of whether the arbitral tribunal set up under UNCLOS or the ECJ was competent to adjudicate the dispute.[18] The same question also arose in the *IJzeren Rijn* or *Iron Rhine* dispute between the Netherlands and Belgium. The parties had established an arbitral tribunal to decide the case, despite the fact that the jurisdiction of the ECJ was obviously

---

10 For a detailed discussion of the *Solange* method see: Lavranos (2008c).

11 BVerfGE 113, 273 *Europäischer Haftbefehl.*

12 See: Herzog / Gerken (2008).

13 See e.g.: Harpaz (2009b); Douglas-Scott (2006a); Dippel (2004); Canor (2000).

14 For a detailed analysis see: Callewaert (2008); Craig / De Búrca (2008).

15 ECrtHR, *Bosphorus v. Ireland*, judgment of 30.6.2005.

16 *Ibid.*, para. 156.

17 See eg: Lavranos (2006b).

18 For details, see: Lavranos (2006e).

relevant.[19] In short, these cases illustrate the fact that the issue of horizontal jurisdictional competition between the ECJ and other international courts and tribunals is becoming increasingly important and thus needs to be addressed.[20]

In addition, and on a more general level, a number of cases involving jurisdictional competition have come up in other configurations between various international courts and tribunals. Besides the ICJ-ICTY debate mentioned above, reference can also be made to the WTO-FTAs nexus, for instance the *Mexico soft drinks* and the *Brazilian Tyres* cases, which involved on the one hand the WTO and on the other hand NAFTA and MERCOSUR dispute settlement bodies respectively.[21]

In other words, jurisdictional competition is a general, widespread phenomenon. Moreover, it is important to note that all these courts and tribunals operate independently and without coordination, i.e. they are not formally bound by each others' jurisprudence. This increases the possibility of divergent or even conflicting rulings on the same legal issues being made. The situation is further complicated by the fact that a heterogeneous picture emerges regarding the way that the various international treaties which have established dispute settlement bodies deal with competing jurisdictions.

Contracting Parties have sometimes regulated the delineation of jurisdiction explicitly and in great detail, but have also often left the issue entirely unregulated. For example, in Article 287 of UNCLOS several dispute settlement bodies are listed ranging from the ICJ, ITLOS, to arbitral tribunals that can be selected according to the preference of the Contracting Parties involved. In other cases, such as in Article 2005 of NAFTA, it is established that once the NAFTA dispute settlement procedure has been selected the WTO dispute settlement procedure is excluded and vice versa.[22] By contrast, Article 292 of the EC Treaty obliges EC Member States to bring any disputes between them (potentially) involving EC law exclusively before the ECJ.[23] Finally, whereas Article 32 ECHR states that the jurisdiction of the ECrtHR shall extend to all matters concerning the interpretation and application of the ECHR and the protocols thereof, it does not explicitly

19 *Ibid.*

20 See generally: Maljean-Dubois (2008).

21 See e.g.: Henckels (2008).

22 Article 2005 NAFTA reads as follows:

1. Subject to paragraphs 2, 3 and 4, disputes regarding any matter arising under both this Agreement and the General Agreement on Tariffs and Trade, any agreement negotiated thereunder, or any successor agreement (GATT), may be settled in either forum at the discretion of the complaining Party.

[...]

6. Once dispute settlement procedures have been initiated under Article 2007 or dispute settlement proceedings have been initiated under the GATT, the forum selected shall be used to the exclusion of the other, unless a Party makes a request pursuant to paragraph 3 or 4.

23 Article 292 EC reads as follows:

Member States undertake not to submit a dispute concerning the interpretation or application of this Treaty to any method of settlement other than those provided for therein.

regulate the situation of competing jurisdiction, for instance arising from the ECJ's case law on fundamental rights.

Hence, the phenomenon of jurisdictional competition raises a whole range of unsettled fundamental questions, both at the international and European law level. Fortunately, over the past few years several important books and articles have been published which have analyzed many relevant aspects. For example, just to mention a few works, reference can be made to the groundbreaking publications of Cesare Romano[24], Yuval Shany[25], Heiko Sauer[26] and Chester Brown[27]. It goes without saying that the present analysis of this topic has greatly benefited from these works.

This book begins in Chapter 2 with a description of the legal framework in which jurisdictional competition has been taking place, both at the international and European law level. Against this background, Chapter 3 will present several detailed case studies that illustrate the various types of competing jurisdiction, their contexts, and the ultimate solutions adopted. In Chapter 4 possible solutions will be discussed, and some general conclusions will be drawn in Chapter 5.

---

[24] Romano (1999).

[25] Shany (OUP 2007); *idem.*, (OUP 2003).

[26] Sauer (2008).

[27] Brown (2007).

CHAPTER 2

The Legal Framework

1 The legal framework

The phenomenon of jurisdictional competition can be attributed to several current parallel developments at the international and European law level. This Chapter aims to provide the legal framework for the subsequent analysis of the case studies by first highlighting developments at the international law level, and then discussing those at the European law level.

1.1 Developments at the international law level

Among the many factors contributing to jurisdictional competition, the proliferation of international courts and tribunals, the institutionalization of international law and the risk of the fragmentation of international law are considered particularly relevant and are thus discussed in more detail below.

1.1.1 The proliferation of international courts and tribunals

Since the early 1990s we have witnessed an indisputable proliferation of international courts and tribunals[28] endowed with the jurisdiction to deal with certain areas of international law or to settle specific disputes, as well as an increase in the willingness of states to use these courts.[29] Reference can be made to bodies such as the International Tribunal for the Law of the Sea (ITLOS), the tribunals for the former Yugoslavia (ICTY) and Rwanda (ICTR), the International Criminal Court (ICC), the internationalized hybrid courts for Sierra Leone, Cambodia, East Timor and Kosovo, the dispute settlement system of the World Trade Organisation (WTO), and the MERCOSUR Permanent Review Court. This development has been spurred by the globalisation of political, legal and economic relations between states, and the increasing involvement of other actors such as international organisations, multinationals and individuals on the international plane.[30] As a result, states, International Organizations (IOs) and private parties that are involved in a dispute can potentially choose from many more dispute settlement bodies than used to previously be the case. Indeed, if one examines the number of judgments delivered by the ICJ in recent years, it becomes apparent that it is being used much more than in the past. Similarly, the dispute settlement system of the WTO has recently been used much more often than under the GATT 1947. Besides, a real explosion in the number of arbitration awards is noticeable, in particular regarding ICSID cases, but also concerning arbitration tribunals established under UNCLOS and the PCA. This overall increase in the use of adjudication and arbitration as a tool for

[28] The term 'international courts and tribunals' is used in a generic way encompassing all kinds of international courts, (arbitral) tribunals and quasi-judicial bodies, established on a permanent, semi-permanent or ad hoc basis.

[29] See in particular: Romano (1999); Martinez (2003).

[30] See e.g.: Kumm (2004); Von Bogdandy (2004).

dispute resolution is a reflection of the on-going shift from power-based towards rule-based dispute resolution.[31] In other words, disputes are increasingly being solved through adjudication and arbitration and on the basis of justice, rather than through the use of arms.[32]

While the creation of an ever increasing number of dispute settlement bodies should as such be welcomed, it can become problematic because the scope of their jurisdictions can potentially overlap. In other words, two or even more courts may simultaneously have jurisdiction to adjudicate the same dispute or parts thereof. The problem is further exacerbated by the fact that all these courts and tribunals act – in principle – completely independently of each other and are not formally bound by each others' decisions. As a result, the proliferation of international courts and tribunals that is currently taking place significantly amplifies jurisdictional competition between the various international courts and tribunals. This in turn can lead to two opposing developments. In the first place, jurisdictional competition can contribute to the institutionalization or even constitutionalization of international law.[33] In the second place, jurisdictional competition can lead to an increasing number of conflicting rulings on the same issues of law, thereby resulting in the fragmentation of international law.[34]

1.1.2 The institutionalization of international law

Since the end of the Cold War in 1989, we have been witnessing a surge in co-operation between nation states, in particular by using previously-established IOs that were paralysed by the Cold War, as was the case with the UN Security Council, as well as through the establishment of new IOs or in other comparable institutionalized settings such as Conferences/Meetings of Parties (COPs/MOPs) within the framework of multilateral environmental agreements (MEAs).[35] Consequently, the growing level of activity of IOs results in an increase in terms of both the quantity and quality of their law making.[36] This development of creating new sources of international law inevitably leads to a higher density of international law, which in turn forms the basis for its greater institutionalization or even constitutionalization.[37] In other words, public international law is increasingly covering all areas of law and providing a common standard or framework for the conduct of states, and also for other subjects of international law such as IOs, multinationals, NGOs and ultimately individuals. Indeed, some regard the level of institutionalization of international

31 See e.g.: Jackson (1998); *idem.*, (1990); (2001); *idem.*, (1999).

32 Petersmann (2008).

33 See further: Peters (2006); De Wet (2006); Burke-White (2004).

34 See: Hafner (2004).

35 See e.g.: Helfer (2008); Lavranos (2002); Churchill / Ulfstein (2000); Röben (2000).

36 See e.g. Alvarez (2005).

37 See further Kumm, *supra* note 30; Rao (2004); Orrego Vicuña (2004) 10 ff.

law to have matured to the point that it could provide the basis for a process of constitutionalization of international law.[38]

In this context, the proliferation of international courts and tribunals and the growing number of judgments and awards that are made can further enhance the density of international law, which in turn can contribute to its institutionalization.[39] In addition, the creation of all these (quasi) judicial bodies – and one should emphasize that new international courts/tribunals continue to be created[40] – also entails increased interaction and communication between their judges, leading possibly to a global community of courts.[41] Moreover, since the judges in these international courts and tribunals often face similar legal problems and have to apply the same rules and principles of international law, they naturally refer to each others' decisions, thereby contributing to the institutionalization of international law.[42] Indeed, the proliferation and diversity of international courts and tribunals is seen by some as a sign of maturity of the international legal system and as a reflection of the growing unity and integrity of international law.[43] This has been the thrust of opinion of several eminent authorities. For example, in 1998 the late Professor Charney in his Hague lectures extensively examined several international courts and tribunals and the potential of conflicting rulings by them.[44] His assumption was that the judges and arbitrators in the various international courts and tribunals more or less apply the same methodology, and thus come to more or less the same application of international law.[45] Consequently, his main conclusion was that the danger of international law fragmenting is very little.[46]

Furthermore, Chester Brown has recently emphasized the growing evidence which points towards a common law of international adjudication, in the sense that there is a convergence between international courts and tribunals regarding the way they handle similar or comparable procedural issues.[47] Accordingly, cross-fertilization of legal principles takes place, which has positive implications for the international legal order.[48]

---

38 See e.g.: Special issue of *LJIL* on Constitutionalism and International Law (2006, issue no. 3); De Wet, *supra* note 33; Cass (2001).

39 See: Orrego Vicuña, *op cit.*

40 For instance, the Permanent Review Court of the MERCOSUR has recently been established. Similarly, also the Caribbean Court of Justice has recently become functional. See with regard to Africa: Pauwelyn (2004).

41 Slaughter (2003); *idem.*, (2000).

42 For a statistical analysis of the interaction between various international courts and tribunals see: Miller (2002).

43 See: Rao, *supra* note 37.

44 Charney (1998).

45 *Ibid.*

46 Charney (2002).

47 See: Brown (2007) *op cit.*

48 *Ibid.*

Moreover, several other authors have also argued that the possible danger of the fragmentation of international law caused by the proliferation of international courts is small, and that the positive aspects clearly outweigh the negative ones.[49]

Hence, according to these writers, the proliferation of international courts and tribunals creates practically no legal problems or legal conflicts. In fact, the above authors argue that the proliferation of international courts and tribunals should be welcomed as the beginning of an emerging global jurisprudence.[50] Consequently, there is little to worry about competing jurisdictions or the possibility that conflicting judgments might be delivered by the various international courts and tribunals.[51]

1.1.3 The risk of fragmentation of international law

While the argument that a global community of courts, and on a more general level that global governance in a world of networks, contributes to the constitutionalization of international law and international relations has been forcefully posited by Anne-Marie Slaughter many times[52], the risk of the fragmentation[53] of international law caused by the very same effect of the proliferation of international courts and tribunals cannot be overlooked and must thus be addressed.[54]

Indeed, the International Law Commission (ILC) found this subject so topical that it commissioned a feasibility report in order to determine its relevancy for further long-term study by the ILC. Professor Hafner presented his report to the ILC in 2000 and came to the conclusion that the danger of fragmentation is at least sufficiently great that it should be explored further by the ILC.[55] The ILC decided on that basis to create a study group chaired by Professor Koskenniemi to analyze the topic further. Unfortunately, the ILC limited the scope of the study group by excluding the aspect of the proliferation of international courts and tribunals and their possible effect on the fragmentation of international law.[56] As a result, the final study report of the ILC published in the summer of

---

49 See e.g.: Buergenthal (2001); Spelliscy (2001); Simma (2004).

50 Slaughter (2004) Chapter 2.

51 *Ibid.*

52 *Ibid.*

53 For a historical overview on the understanding of fragmentation see: Martineau (2009).

54 See e.g.: Hafner (2000); *idem.*, (2004); Schwebel (1999); Guillaume (2000); Koskenniemi (2004); Dupuy (1999); *idem.*, (2007a); *idem.*, (2007b).

55 Hafner, *supra* note 54.

56 Report of the Study Group on Fragmentation of International law: Difficulties arising from the Diversification and Expansion of International Law, ILC, 55th A/CN.4/L.644, 18.7.2003.

2006 does not unfortunately discuss the institutional aspects of jurisdictional competition between international courts and tribunals.[57]

Nonetheless, subsequent studies by Professor Shany[58], Heiko Sauer[59] and the present writer[60] demonstrate that the negative effects associated with competing jurisdictions are actually quite real, as is also illustrated by the case studies discussed in more detail in the next Chapter. These concerns are supported by several other authors who point to the danger that the coherence of international law could be threatened by a possible divergence between the jurisprudence of the different international courts and tribunals, which could lead to its fragmentation.[61] These authors emphasize the persistent shortcomings of the various international courts and tribunals, and the fragmented legal framework in which they have to operate and interact.[62]

However, the present contribution will argue that the really crucial systemic shortcoming within international law is the lack of a legal hierarchy (with the exception of *jus cogens* norms and Article 103 UN Charter, claiming primacy over other norms of international law) generally, and the lack of legal hierarchy between all the various international courts and tribunals specifically. Thus, it is quite possible that a dispute involving the same legal question or legal norm is interpreted and applied by two different international courts in very different – possibly conflicting – ways.[63] Indeed, a well-known example is the occasional divergent jurisprudence that exists between the ECJ and the European Court of Human Rights (ECrtHR) regarding the interpretation and application of fundamental rights as protected by the European Convention on Human Rights (ECHR).[64] The lack of a clear explicit hierarchical determination of which court should have the last word regarding European fundamental rights has lead to several divergent judgments by both courts on similar issues.[65]

Similarly, the phenomenon of divergent or conflicting jurisprudence is also quite common at the national law level. However, the difference is that at the end of the day there will be one supreme arbiter, a supreme court or a constitutional court, which will determine the dispute *in fine* with a judgement which is binding for the parties and often also binding for the other lower domestic courts.

Likewise, the relationship between the ECJ and the national courts of the EC Member States is regulated hierarchically by putting the ECJ at the top

---

57 Report of the Study Group of the ILC, Fragmentation of International law: Difficulties arising from the Diversification and Expansion of International Law, ILC 58th session, A/CN/4.L702, 18.7.2006, para. 8.

58 Shany, *supra* note 25.

59 Sauer, *supra* note 26.

60 Lavranos (2005b).

61 See: Schwebel; Guilliaume; Dupuy, *op cit.*

62 Alvarez (2003); Hafner, *op cit.*

63 See extensively: Shany, *op cit.*

64 See: Young (2005); Canor, *supra* note 13; Spielmann (1999).

65 See for details: Lavranos (2004) Chapter 4; Spielmann, *op cit.*

of the hierarchy. Despite the fact that the ECJ describes its relationship with the national courts as one of 'co-operation', when it comes in particular to the preliminary reference procedure of Article 234 EC, ECJ judgments are final and binding for the national courts requesting preliminary rulings from it.[66] Indeed, due to the supremacy of Community law over all national law, and combined with the obligation of EC Member States to do everything in order to give full effect to EC law and to refrain from opposing its full effect in any way (Article 10 EC), the judgments of the ECJ are *de facto* binding on all national courts of the EC Member States.[67] It is precisely the lack of this kind of explicit and formal regulation of the jurisdictional relationship at the international level which makes the issue of competing jurisdictions so urgent.

The previous Chapter has clearly illustrated the fact that the globalization of international law results in many different developments – sometimes seemingly opposing ones. On the one hand, a continuing institutionalization of international law through the establishment of more international courts and tribunals and the production of an increasing amount of case law by those courts is taking place. On the other hand – and at the same time – the proliferation of international courts and tribunals and the increasing number of their decisions and awards increases the chances of conflicting rulings, which in turn augments the risk of fragmentation of international law. This is particularly the case because of the lack of a binding legal hierarchy between the norms of international law, and between the various international courts and tribunals. As a consequence, there are currently no formal mechanisms in place – such as for instance the preliminary ruling system within the Community legal order – which could ensure that the on-going institutionalization of international law is accompanied by a hierarchization, or at least co-ordination, between the various international courts and tribunals and their decisions.

2 Developments at the European law level

At the European law level, two interconnected developments are relevant to note regarding the jurisdiction of the ECJ. First, there is the on-going expansion of the EC's external relations into a growing number of policy areas.[68] As a result, the EC has become party to innumerable international agreements and member of countless IOs – many of which provide for their own dispute

---

[66] See further: Martinico / Fontanelli (2008); Komarek (2005).

[67] Whereas the supremacy and binding effect of ECJ judgments is not explicitly stated in the EC Treaty and therefore is disputed, recent ECJ jurisprudence provides a sufficient basis for such an assumption. See e.g.: Case C-453/00 *Kühne & Heitz* [2004] ECR I-837; Case C-224/01 *Köbler* [2003] ECR I-10239. See also: Chalmers (2006) 295-296; and for a more theoretical conceptual analysis: Meyer (2006).

[68] On the external relations of the EU generally see: Koutrakos (2006); Eeckhout (2004); Lavranos, *supra* note 65.

settlement system.[69] Moreover, it should be recalled that according to the jurisprudence of the ECJ, all international obligations that are binding on the EC become integral parts of the Community legal order, i.e. are 'communitarized'.[70] Second, since the jurisdiction of the ECJ and Court of First Instance (CFI) runs parallel to the competence of the EC, the expansion of the EC's external competence into areas that used to be predominantly regulated by international law also results in an equal expansion of the jurisdiction of the ECJ/CFI. In other words, the ECJ/CFI are increasingly called upon to adjudicate international law issues, which in turn results in an overlap with the jurisdiction of the other international courts and tribunals.

In order to assess the extent to which the jurisdiction of the ECJ overlaps with the jurisdiction of other international courts and tribunals, it is crucial to first identify the ECJ's scope of jurisdiction regarding international treaties.

2.1 The scope of ECJ jurisdiction regarding international treaties

The scope of jurisdiction of the ECJ/CFI can be summarized as follows.[71] In the first place, the jurisdiction of the ECJ/CFI extends to international treaties concluded on the basis of an explicit exclusive competence of the EC. For instance, Articles 133 and 310 EC are two of the very few explicit provisions of the EC Treaty which give the EC exclusive external competence to sign international agreements, for example tariff and trade agreements and association agreements, with third states.[72] Besides, the Treaty of Nice substantially amended Article 133 EC by including certain agreements on trade in services and commercial aspects of intellectual property rights.[73] Consequently, the ECJ's jurisdiction extends to all the areas covered by the agreements falling within the scope of Articles 133 and 310 EC.

In the second place, the jurisdiction of the ECJ/CFI covers international treaties concluded on the basis of an internal competence of the EC (the so-called *AETR*-doctrine).[74] The *AETR*-doctrine[75] developed by the ECJ states that whenever the EC has promulgated Community legislation in one policy area, it automatically acquires exclusive external competence in that field. Obviously, this has resulted in an enormous expansion of the EC's activities on the international plane, especially through the ratification of numerous international

---

69 See e.g.: Oen (2005).

70 See e.g.: Opinion AG Kokott in Case C-308/06 *Intertanko* [2008] ECR I-4057; Lavranos, *supra* note 65.

71 It should be noted that the scope of jurisdiction of the ECJ also to some degree compromises international treaties concluded under the II and III pillars of the EU Treaty, which, however, will not be discussed in this book. For an analysis see: Lavranos (2008a).

72 See for details: Vranes (2009); Eeckhout (2004).

73 See: Herrmann (2002).

74 On the *AETR*-doctrine see: Eeckhout, *op cit.*

75 Case 22/70 *AETR* [1971] ECR 263.

agreements and membership of many IOs.[76] However, starting with its Opinion 1/94[77] on the WTO Agreement and subsequently in its open-skies judgment[78], the ECJ substantially restricted the *AETR*-doctrine by ruling that the competence of the EC becomes exclusive only *after* a certain policy area has been fully, or at least to a large extent, harmonized by EC legislation. Consequently, one would assume that the expansion of the external competence of the EC has come to a halt, but rather the contrary is true. Indeed, in its Opinion 1/03[79] on the new Lugano Convention, the ECJ seems to have relaxed its stance and has returned to its *AETR*-formula. In any case, the EC has over the past decade obtained many new competences that can become exclusive external ones as soon as sufficient harmonizing legislation has been issued.[80]

In the third place, the jurisdiction of the ECJ/CFI also covers so-called mixed agreements, i.e. concluded by both the EC and its Member States.[81] The specific characteristic of mixed agreements is that they touch partly on the competence of the EC and partly on the competence of the Member States, which implies that the EC is only competent for its part, while the Member States remain competent for their part. However, the ECJ has used the argument of ensuring the uniform application of mixed agreements to interpret its jurisdiction very broadly.[82] Accordingly, it can be concluded that the jurisdiction of the ECJ and CFI extends to all the provisions of a mixed agreement except those that fall within the exclusive competence of the Member States.[83]

In the fourth place, the jurisdiction of the ECJ/CFI can even extend to treaties concluded by EC Member States alone. Whereas in principle these treaties, if they do not fall within the exclusive competence of the EC, are outside the scope of Community law and thus outside the jurisdiction of the ECJ, there are two cases in which the ECJ exerts a sort of 'implied jurisdiction' over them. The first example is the former GATT 1947 and the second example is the European Convention on Human Rights (ECHR). Regarding the GATT 1947, it should be noted that the EC was never a contracting party to it. However, because the GATT 1947 fell within the exclusive competence of the EC (former Article 113 EC, now Article 133 EC), the ECJ was able to extend its jurisdiction due to the fact that the EC *de facto* replaced the Member States as regards the GATT 1947.[84] Similarly, regarding the ECHR, the EC has never been a contracting party to it, while all EC Member States are. Nevertheless, the ECJ incorpo-

76 See extensively: Eeckhout, *op cit.*

77 Opinion 1/94 *WTO Agreement* [1994] ECR I-5267.

78 See further: Franklin (2005); Lavranos (2003).

79 Opinion 1/03 *Lugano Convention* [2006] ECR I-1145.

80 See further: Baumé (2006); Lavranos (2006a).

81 Heliskoski (2001).

82 See: Case 104/81 *Kupferberg* [1982] ECR 3641; Case C-61/94 *Commission v. Germany* [1996] ECR I-3989.

83 Koutrakos (2002); Dashwood (2000).

84 Case 21-24/72 *International Fruit Company* [1972] ECR 1219.

rated the ECHR through its case law into the Community legal order.[85] Indeed, the ECJ has been applying the ECHR directly[86] and has accepted that the ECHR can be used as a justification for the EC Member States to even restrict the four 'internal market' freedoms (free movement of goods, workers, services and capital) guaranteed by the EC Treaty.[87] Hence, over time the ECJ has integrated the ECHR into the Community legal order and thus seized jurisdiction to interpret and apply it when Community law is involved.[88]

However, it should be noted that in its more recent case law, the ECJ has been less inclined to extend its jurisdiction to international agreements, more specifically international environmental agreements, to which the EC is not a contracting party and where the EC has not (yet) *de facto* replaced the Member States by acquiring full competence in the policy area concerned.[89]

2.2 The exclusive scope of jurisdiction of the ECJ under Article 292 EC

Apart from determining the scope of jurisdiction of the ECJ on the basis of the external competence of the EC, Article 292 EC is highly relevant for our purposes. It states that[90]:

> 'Member States undertake not to submit a dispute concerning the interpretation or application of this Treaty to any method of settlement other than those provided for therein.'

Before the *MOX plant* judgment[91] was issued by the ECJ in 2006, the ECJ touched only once on Article 292 EC, when it issued its Opinion 1/91 on the establishment of a court for the European Economic Area (EEA).[92] Regarding the scope of jurisdiction of the EEA court and the impact on the exclusive jurisdiction of the ECJ, the ECJ argued that the jurisdiction of the EEA court would adversely affect the allocation of responsibilities defined in the EC Treaty, and ultimately would upset the autonomy of the Community legal order.[93] For these reasons the ECJ declared the jurisdiction conferred to the EEA court incompat-

85 See e.g.: Case 4/73 *Nold* [1974] ECR 491; Case C-260/89 *ERT* [1991] ECR I-2925.

86 See e.g.: Case C-413/99 *Baumbast* [2002] ECR I-7091; Case C-60/00 *Carpenter* [2002] ECR I-6279; Case C-117/01 *K.B.* [2004] ECR I-541; Case C-200/02 *Chen* [2004] ECR I-9925.

87 Case C-112/00 *Schmidberger* [2003] ECR I-5659; see further: Gonzales (2004).

88 See: N. Lavranos, *supra* note 65, Chapter 4.

89 See e.g.: Case C-188/07 *Commune de Mesquer* [2008] ECR I-4501; Case C-308/06 *Intertanko* [2008] ECR I-4057. See generally: Wennerås (2008).

90 A similarly worded provision can be found in Article 193 Euratom.

91 Case C-459/03 *Commission v. Ireland* [2006] ECR I-4635. See further: Romano (2007); Lavranos (2007).

92 Opinion 1/91 *EEA* [1991] ECR I-6079.

93 *Ibid.*, para. 35.

ible with Community law. In the *MOX plant* judgment, the ECJ used similar language, concluding that

> '154. It must also be pointed out that the institution and pursuit of proceedings before the Arbitral Tribunal, in the circumstances indicated in paragraphs 146 to 150 of the present judgment, involve *a manifest risk that the jurisdictional order* laid down in the Treaties and, consequently, the *autonomy of the Community legal system may be adversely affected*.'[94] [emphasis added].

Also, more recently, in the *Kadi* judgment[95] the ECJ underlined that

> '282. It is also to be recalled that *an international agreement cannot affect the allocation of powers fixed by the Treaties or, consequently, the autonomy of the Community legal system, observance of which is ensured by the Court by virtue of the exclusive jurisdiction conferred on it by Article 220 EC, jurisdiction that the Court has, moreover, already held to form part of the very foundations of the Community* (see, to that effect, Opinion 1/91 [1991] ECR I-6079, paragraphs 35 and 71, and Case C-459/03 Commission v Ireland [2006] ECR I-4635, paragraph 123 and case law cited).' [emphasis added].

Obviously, from the point of view of Community law, and in particular from the point of view of the ECJ, it is understandable that the ECJ is interpreting Article 292 EC in such a broad fashion. It is apparently concerned about the increased possibility that other international courts and tribunals be put in a position to interpret and apply Community law. Its exclusive jurisdiction is coming under pressure from the ongoing proliferation of international courts and tribunals as well as the expanding external relations activities of the EC and its Member States. As a consequence, the ECJ is increasingly called upon to interpret international law aspects that have become integral parts of the Community legal order at a time when a growing number of international courts and tribunals are being created and exercise their jurisdiction in areas of international law that are also regulated by EC law. This increasingly results in jurisdictional overlap between the ECJ and other international courts and tribunals, which in the eyes of the ECJ poses a possible threat to its exclusive jurisdiction to interpret and apply Community law.

3 Summary

This Chapter has illustrated several developments at both the international and European law level that contribute to the various effects asso-

---

[94] Case C-459/03 *Commission v. Ireland* [2006] ECR I-4635.

[95] Joined Cases C-402/05 P and C-415/05 P *Kadi* and *Al Barakaat International Foundation*, judgment of the ECJ of 3.9.2008. See further: Gattini (2009); G. Harpaz (2009a); Lavranos (2009c).

ciated with competing jurisdictions. In short, the proliferation of international courts and tribunals can either contribute to the institutionalisation of international law or else increase the risk of its fragmentation. These contrasting developments are further exacerbated by the heterogeneous approach of international agreements regarding the way they deal with competing jurisdictions. Some agreements offer a menu of options for selecting a dispute settlement body, some prescribe the exclusive jurisdiction of one court, while others still are simply silent on the issue. Hence, as is also illustrated by the case studies discussed in the following Chapter, so far no generally accepted approach to competing jurisdiction has been developed. In contrast, the ECJ has taken a very clear stance in protecting its exclusive jurisdiction to the maximum possible extent. Moreover, due to the continuously expanding jurisdiction of the ECJ into matters of international law, it increasingly interferes in the exercise of jurisdiction of the other international courts and tribunals.

In summary, the proliferation of international courts and tribunals, coupled with the expansion of the scope of jurisdiction of the ECJ into more international law areas, inevitably means that these courts and tribunals must regulate, or at least coordinate, their position on whether or not to exercise jurisdiction in a given situation if they want to perform their task of resolving disputes effectively and efficiently, and retain their authority.

CHAPTER 3

Case Studies

1 Introduction

In this Chapter several case studies will be discussed in more detail in order to demonstrate the practical problems that have arisen from competing jurisdictions. These cases cover a wide range of different courts and tribunals and different legal areas, illustrating both the commonalties and differences in the way competing international jurisdictions have been dealt with.

The first case that will be discussed is the *MOX plant* dispute, which arouse between Ireland and the UK concerning the radioactive emissions of the nuclear power station situated in Sellafield, UK. This environmental law case revolved around the question of whether the UK violated its obligations under the UNCLOS and OSPAR treaties. The dispute was brought before two arbitral tribunals, one set up under UNCLOS and the other under OSPAR, as well as the ECJ. Since this dispute involved EC environmental law as well as UNCLOS and OSPAR treaty provisions, the central jurisdictional question was whether or not the dispute should have been brought exclusively before the ECJ.

The second case concerns the *IJzeren Rijn* or *Iron Rhine* dispute between the Netherlands and Belgium. *Prima facie*, this case revolved around the question of which of the two countries should pay for the reactivation of an old railway track, called Iron Rhine, which runs from Antwerp harbour, through the Netherlands into Germany. However, since the EC Habitat Directive had to be applied, the real issue of the case was whether the parties were allowed to bring the case before an international ad hoc arbitral tribunal or whether they were obliged to let the ECJ decide the dispute.

The third case to be discussed is the *Mexico soft drinks* dispute between Mexico and the US. Both countries had for several years been involved in a dispute on the import and export of sugar and sugar substitutes, which are *inter alia* also used in soft drinks. Among other things, this dispute raised the jurisdictional competition issue between the NAFTA and WTO dispute settlement systems. Mexico had argued that the WTO panel and Appellate Body should not exercise their jurisdiction in this case because the dispute was actually part of a wider NAFTA dispute between Mexico and the US. Therefore, according to Mexico, a NAFTA panel would be better placed to adjudicate the case.

The fourth case continues the jurisdictional competition issue within the WTO-RTA nexus, but this time in the guise of the *Brazilian Tyres* case, which involved MERCOSUR and WTO dispute settlement bodies. The case revolved around the justification of Brazil's import ban on retreaded tyres – both under MERCOSUR and WTO trade rules – in order to curb the spread of dengue fever.

The fifth case will focus on the issue of competing jurisdiction between the ICJ and the ICTY. A couple of years ago, the ICTY, when faced with the question of defining state and subsequently individual responsibility, considered it necessary to explicitly deviate from the ICJ's long standing 'effective control test' as established in its *Nicaragua* judgment by applying a less stringent 'overall control test'. However, in its recent *Genocide Convention* judgment, the ICJ flatly rejected the ICTY's approach and indeed refused to accept that the ICTY has any jurisdiction to redefine the 'effective control test'.

Finally, the sixth case will turn to the *Bosphorus* judgment of the ECrtHR. The *Bosporus* case concerned the legality of measures adopted by Ireland for the purpose of implementing sanctions imposed by the UN Security Council against the FRY, which were also transposed by EC Regulations. The case was first decided by the ECJ responding to preliminary questions from the Irish Supreme Court. Subsequently, Bosphorus brought the case before the ECrtHR. In this case, the ECrtHR was basically called upon to review the prior *Bosphorus* judgment of the ECJ. In other words, the ECrtHR was essentially asked to define the scope of its jurisdiction vis-à-vis the ECJ concerning fundamental rights cases that arise within the context of the implementation of EC law measures by Contracting Parties of the ECHR which also happen to be EC Member States.

All case studies are first introduced by sketching out the factual and legal background. This is followed by a synthesis of the jurisdictional issues discussed in the various (quasi) judicial decisions, and then a commentary.

2 The *MOX plant* dispute

2.1 The factual and legal background

For many years Ireland has been concerned about radioactive discharges from the MOX plant situated in Sellafield UK that were being released into the Irish Sea.[96] After having unsuccessfully tried to obtain information from the UK about the discharges from the plant, Ireland instituted proceedings against the UK by raising two different claims.[97] First, Ireland wanted to obtain from the UK all the available information regarding the radioactive discharges of the MOX plant using Article 9 of the Convention for the Protection of the Marine Environment of the North-East Atlantic (OSPAR). Article 9(2) OSPAR requires the Contracting Parties to make available information 'on the state of the maritime area, on activities or measures adversely affecting or likely to affect it'. Second, Ireland believed that the discharges from the MOX plant radioactively contaminated its waters and therefore constituted a violation of the UN Law of the Sea Convention (UNCLOS). Accordingly, it sought an award for the disclosure of information regarding the MOX plant from the UK on the basis of the OSPAR convention and also a declaration that the UK had violated its obligations under UNCLOS. After lengthy negotiations, Ireland and the UK agreed to establish arbitral tribunals under both – the OSPAR and UNCLOS – conventions in order to resolve the dispute.

---

96 For an overview see: Brazel (2006).

97 For the materials of the dispute see: Permanent Court of Arbitration, available at: www.pca-cpa.org. See further: Shany (2004); Churchill / Scott (2004).

The issue of jurisdictional competition in this case comes into play because of the existence of relevant EC environmental legislation (and EURATOM) and the fact that the dispute was between two EC Member States. As explained in the previous Chapter, Article 292 EC requires EC Member States to bring disputes that potentially involve EC law exclusively before the ECJ. Accordingly, this case *inter alia* raised the question of whether the jurisdictions of the arbitral tribunals established under UNCLOS and OSPAR overlap with the jurisdiction of the ECJ, and, if so, what the consequences are and how the courts and tribunals involved should deal with them.

2.2 The various judicial decisions on the *MOX plant* dispute

2.2.1 The OSPAR Arbitral Tribunal Award

In its decision of 2 July 2003 the OSPAR arbitral tribunal asserted its jurisdiction and rendered a final award.[98] As regards the possible implications of EC law, the OSPAR arbitral tribunal refused to take into account any other sources of international law or European law that might potentially be applicable in the dispute. Whereas Article 32(5)(a) of OSPAR states that the arbitral tribunal shall decide according to the 'rules of international law, and, in particular those of the [OSPAR] Convention', the OSPAR arbitral tribunal argued that the OSPAR Convention had to be considered to be a 'self-contained' dispute settlement regime, so that the tribunal could base its decision only on the OSPAR Convention.[99] In other words, the OSPAR arbitral tribunal did not consider itself to be competent to take into account other relevant sources of international or European law (in particular EC Directive 90/313[100], replaced by EC Directive 2003/4[101]), relevant ECJ jurisprudence[102] or the Convention on access to information, public participation in decision-making, and access to justice regarding environmental matters (Aarhus Convention) of 1998, which has been ratified by all EC Member States and recently also by the EC itself.[103]

In substance, the OSPAR Arbitral Tribunal decided that the UK had not violated its obligations under OSPAR by not disclosing the information sought

98 OSPAR Arbitral Tribunal, *MOX plant*, final award. See further: McDorman / Caron (2004).

99 OSPAR Arbitral Tribunal, *MOX plant*, final award, para. 143.

100 Council Directive 90/313/EEC of 7.6.1990 on the freedom of access to information on the environment [1990] OJ L 158/56.

101 Directive 2003/4 of the EP and of the Council of 28.1.2003 on public access to environmental information and repealing Council Directive 90/313/EEC [2003] OJ L 41/26.

102 See e.g.: Case C-186/04 *Housieaux* [2005] ECR I-3299; Case C-233/00 *Commission v. France* [2003] ECR I-6625; Case C-316/01 *Glawischnig* [2003] ECR I-5995; Case C-217/97 *Commission v. Germany* [1999] ECR I-5087; Case C-321/96 *Wilhelm Mecklenburg v. Kreis Pinneberg – Der Landrat* [1998] ECR I-3809.

103 Council Decision 2005/370/EC of 17.2.2005 on the conclusion, on behalf of the EC, of the Convention on access to information, public participation in decision-making and access to justice in environmental matters [2005] OJ L 124/1. See generally: De Abreu Ferreira (2008).

by Ireland. It did not deal at all with the implications of the potential exclusive jurisdiction of the ECJ based on Article 292 EC, but rather rendered its award by applying a narrowly-defined interpretation of its own jurisdiction, which in its view prevented it from taking other sources of law into account. Of course, the OSPAR Arbitral Tribunal was not legally obliged to take Community law or the relevant ECJ jurisprudence into account. However, by interpreting the disclosure obligations of the UK under OSPAR less strictly than the ECJ does under similar EC law provisions, the OPSAR Arbitral Tribunal created conflicting rights and obligations emanating from two different sources for the parties involved. As a result, the uniform and consistent interpretation and application of the relevant provisions was undermined by its award, which in turn has a fragmentary effect on the legal orders involved.

2.2.2 The UNCLOS Arbitral Tribunal Award

In contrast to the straight-forward OSPAR proceeding, the UNCLOS proceeding appeared to be more complicated because of the various dispute settlement options available. More specifically, Articles 287 and 288 UNCLOS provide that various fora can be selected by the contracting parties to settle their disputes. Parties can use the International Tribunal for the Law of the Sea (ITLOS), the International Court of Justice (ICJ) or ad hoc arbitral tribunals. Moreover, Article 282 UNCLOS explicitly recognizes the possibility of bringing a dispute before dispute settlement bodies established by regional or bilateral agreements.

As the parties had not jointly designated a certain dispute settlement forum, the dispute had to be submitted to an arbitral tribunal in accordance with Annex VII Article 287(5) UNCLOS. However, pending the establishment of this ad hoc arbitral tribunal, Ireland requested interim measures under Article 290(5) UNCLOS from ITLOS. It asked that the UK be ordered to suspend the authorisation of the MOX plant or at least instantly take all measures to stop the operation of the plant. Regarding the issue of jurisdiction, the ITLOS determined that *prima facie* the conditions of Article 290(5) UNCLOS were met so that the Annex VII arbitral tribunal had jurisdiction to decide on the merits of the case.[104] Concerning the substance, the ITLOS ordered both parties to co-operate and enter into consultations regarding the operation of the MOX plant and its emissions into the Irish Sea, pending the decision on the merits of the arbitral award.[105]

After the matter had come before the UNCLOS Arbitral Tribunal, it confirmed the finding of ITLOS that it had *prima facie* jurisdiction.[106] However, in a second step, it considered it necessary to determine whether it indeed

[104] ITLOS, *MOX plant*, Request for Provisional Measures, Order of 3.12.2001.

[105] *Ibid.*

[106] UNCLOS Arbitral Tribunal, *MOX plant*, Suspension of Proceedings on Jurisdiction and Merits and Request for further Provisional Measures, Order No. 3 of 24.6.2003.

had *definite* jurisdiction to solve the dispute, in view of the UK's objection that the ECJ had jurisdiction in this case on the basis of Article 292 EC because Community law was also at issue. The Arbitral Tribunal accepted the UK's objection and consequently stayed the proceedings. Accordingly, it requested the parties to first find out whether or not the ECJ had jurisdiction before it would proceed with rendering a decision on the merits of the case.[107]

The parties did not however have to take any action, as the European Commission (supported by the UK) started an Article 226 EC infringement procedure against Ireland for violating Article 292 EC and the identical provision in the Euratom Treaty. The Commission argued that Ireland had instituted the proceedings against the UK without taking due account of the fact that the EC was a party to UNCLOS. In particular, the Commission claimed that by submitting the dispute to a tribunal outside the Community legal order, Ireland had violated the exclusive jurisdiction of the ECJ as enshrined in Article 292 EC and the similarly-worded Article 193 Euratom. Furthermore, according to the Commission, Ireland had also violated the duty of loyal co-operation incumbent on it under Article 10 EC and the similarly-worded Article 192 Euratom. In this way the *MOX plant* case, at least as far as concerned the UNCLOS proceeding, ultimately came before the ECJ.

2.2.3 The Opinion of Advocate-General Maduro of the ECJ

In his opinion Advocate-General Maduro essentially followed the arguments of the Commission.[108] Accordingly, he rejected Ireland's argument that when the EC ratified UNLCOS and thereby incorporated it into the Community legal order, the Community judicial system was altered by the UNCLOS dispute settlement system. AG Maduro stressed that Article 292 EC prevents any alteration of the ECJ's exclusive jurisdiction regarding the interpretation and application of EC law by an international agreement.[109] Moreover, since Ireland asked the UNCLOS Arbitral Tribunal to interpret and apply UNCLOS provisions that have become an integral part of Community law, Ireland essentially requested the UNCLOS Arbitral Tribunal to interpret and apply Community law.[110] In the opinion of AG Maduro this constituted a violation of the obligations under Article 292 EC.[111] Finally, AG Maduro accepted the Commission's argument that Article 10 EC imposes a mutual duty of sincere cooperation on the EC institutions and the Member States. More specifically, this duty required Ireland to consult with the Commission in order to avoid the risk of infringing Community rules or obstructing Community policies. This duty was particularly crucial in a case such as the present one that involved two

[107] *Ibid.*

[108] Opinion AG Maduro in case C-459/03 *Commission v. Ireland* [2006] ECR I-4635.

[109] *Ibid.*, para. 41.

[110] *Ibid.*, para. 51.

[111] *Ibid.*, para. 52.

EC Member States and an international agreement that had also been ratified by the EC.[112]

In sum, AG Maduro had no difficulty in concluding that Ireland had violated its obligations arising out of Article 292 EC by bringing the dispute before the UNCLOS Arbitral Tribunal.

2.2.4 The *MOX plant* judgment of the ECJ

The starting point of the ECJ's analysis was the question of whether or not this dispute fell within the acting competence of the EC, because only if that were the case would the exclusive jurisdiction of the ECJ based on Article 292 EC have been triggered.[113] From the outset it should be noted that the EC and its Member States concluded UNCLOS as a mixed agreement.[114] In this context the ECJ reaffirmed that mixed agreements have the same status in the Community legal order as agreements concluded by the EC alone.[115] Consequently, when the EC ratified UNCLOS, it became an integral part of the Community legal order.[116] Based on that, the ECJ examined whether the EC had exercised its competence in the policy area (maritime pollution) that was at the centre of the dispute between Ireland and the UK. It concluded that the matters covered by the UNCLOS provisions which Ireland relied on before the Arbitral Tribunal were 'very largely' regulated by Community law.[117] Ireland before the UNCLOS Arbitral Tribunal was therefore relying on provisions that had become part of the Community legal order. Accordingly, the ECJ concluded that the jurisdiction of the ECJ based on Article 292 EC was triggered. The next issue was to determine whether that jurisdiction is indeed exclusive in view of the fact that UNCLOS provides for its own sophisticated dispute settlement system. Referring to its position in Opinion 1/91, the ECJ held that

> '[...] an international agreement cannot affect the allocation of responsibilities defined in the Treaties and, consequently, the autonomy of the Community legal system, compliance with which the Court ensures under Article 220 EC. That exclusive competence is confirmed by Article 292 EC [...].'[118]

---

[112] *Ibid.*, paras. 57-58.

[113] Case C-459/03 *Commission v. Ireland* [2006] ECR I-4635. See for detailed analysis: Romano (2007); Maljean-Dubois / Martin (2007); Adam (2007); Lavranos (2006d).

[114] Council Decision 98/392/EEC of 23.3.1998 concerning the conclusion by the EC of the UN Convention of 10.12.1982 on the Law of the Sea and the Agreement of 28.7.1994 relating to the implementation of Part XI thereof [1998] OJ L 179/1.

[115] Case C-459/03 *Commission v. Ireland*, para. 84.

[116] See also: Case C-308/06 *Intertanko* [2008] ECR I-4057.

[117] Case C-459/03 *Commission v. Ireland*, para. 110.

[118] *Ibid.*, para. 123.

As a consequence thereof, the ECJ reaffirmed that an international agreement such as UNCLOS cannot affect the exclusive jurisdiction of the ECJ regarding the resolution of disputes between Member States concerning the interpretation and application of Community law.[119] Hence, Ireland was precluded on the basis of Articles 292 and 220 EC from bringing the dispute before the UNCLOS arbitral tribunal. Indeed, the ECJ went so far as to state that

> '[...] the institution and pursuit of proceedings before the arbitral tribunal [...], *involve a manifest risk that the jurisdictional order* laid down in the Treaties, consequently, *the autonomy of the Community legal system may be adversely affected.*'[120]

The ECJ did not stop at claiming exclusive jurisdiction in this case, but also found it necessary to make two important further remarks. First, that it is only for the ECJ itself to determine – should the need arise – whether, and if so to what extent, provisions of an international agreement in question fall outside its jurisdiction, and therefore may be adjudicated by another dispute settlement body.[121] Accordingly, if Member States doubt whether a dispute involves Community law aspects, they are essentially obliged to obtain an answer from the ECJ before bringing the case to another dispute settlement body. Second, the ECJ found that Article 292 EC must be understood as a specific expression of the more general duty of loyalty of Member States as enshrined in Article 10 EC.[122] Thus, Member States have a duty to inform and consult with the competent Community institutions (i.e. the Commission and/or the ECJ) prior to bringing a case before a dispute settlement body other than the ECJ.[123] In this way, the Commission and eventually the ECJ are informed in time of a dispute settlement procedure that might interfere with Article 292 EC.

Thus, the ECJ solved the jurisdictional competition issue with regard to the UNCLOS arbitral tribunal by claiming exclusive jurisdiction, which effectively removed the dispute from the jurisdiction of the UNCLOS arbitral tribunal. Indeed, as a result of the ECJ judgment, the UNCLOS arbitral tribunal recently terminated the case.[124]

---

119 *Ibid.*, para. 132.

120 *Ibid.*, para. 154 [emphasis added].

121 *Ibid.*, para. 135.

122 *Ibid.*, para. 169: 'The obligation devolving on Member States, set out in Article 292 EC, to have recourse to the Community judicial system and to respect the Court's exclusive jurisdiction, which is a fundamental feature of that system, must be understood as a specific expression of Member States' more general duty of loyalty resulting from Article 10 EC.'

123 *Ibid.*, para. 179.

124 UNCLOS Arbitral Tribunal, *MOX plant*, Order No. 6, Termination of proceedings, 6.6.2008.

2.3 Commentary

The *MOX plant* dispute for the first time forced the ECJ to explicitly discuss the issue of competing jurisdiction with another international arbitral tribunal, and define the scope of its own. Unsurprisingly, the ECJ used this opportunity to set the tone by vehemently defending its exclusive jurisdiction to the maximum extent. The ECJ is apparently very much concerned that the uniformity and consistency of the interpretation and application of Community law might be endangered if EC Member States start to bring cases that potentially involve EC law aspects before other international courts and tribunals.

While this concern is understandable, it at the same time significantly limits the ability of EC Member States to use other dispute settlement systems of their choice. Moreover, the expansive interpretation of the ECJ's own exclusive jurisdiction inevitably restricts the other international courts and tribunals from exercising their jurisdiction in cases that involve EC Member States and potentially EC law. In fact, the ECJ has essentially conditioned the exercise of the jurisdiction of other international courts and tribunals upon its own prior explicit consent that indeed its exclusive jurisdiction is not affected in any particular case.

Whereas the ECJ was successful with this strategy regarding the UNCLOS Arbitral Tribunal, the limits of the strategy became apparent in the attitude of the OSPAR Arbitral Tribunal, which did not even discuss the possible implications of Article 292 EC and the possible overlap of its jurisdiction with that of the ECJ.

Finally, it is also interesting to note that neither the ECJ nor the UNCLOS Arbitral Tribunal discussed the substance of the dispute, which is quite remarkable considering the fact that several years have passed by and two different dispute settlement bodies have wasted enormous resources in dealing with it. In other words, the question of whether or not the UK violated its UNCLOS obligations has still not been answered – neither from the perspective of UNCLOS provisions nor from the perspective of EC law.[125] Clearly, this is a very disappointing result in terms of efficient and effective dispute resolution and, ultimately, of delivering justice.

3 The *IJzeren Rijn* dispute

3.1 The factual and legal background

In the *IJzeren Rijn* (also known as *Iron Rhine*) case, Belgium and the Netherlands disagreed over who should pay the costs of the reactivation of an old railway line, called the Iron Rhine. The IJzeren Rijn railway line was one of the first international railway lines in mainland Europe in the 19th

[125] See for a more detailed discussion: Lavranos (2009b).

century, running from Antwerp through the Netherlands to the Rhine basin area in Germany. Belgium had a right of transit through the Netherlands on the basis of two treaties dating back to 1839 (Treaty of Separation) and 1897 (Railway Convention). After 1991, the railway line fell into disuse. In the meantime, the Netherlands had designated an area (the Meinweg, close to the city of Roermond), which the railway line crosses, as a 'special area of conservation' according to the EC Habitats Directive. Moreover, in 1994 the Netherlands had also identified the Meinweg as a special protection area in accordance with the EC Birds Directive. However, the Birds Directive was superseded by the EC Habitats Directive as far as is relevant to the present dispute. In addition, the Meinweg area was identified as a national park and as a 'silent area' under Dutch domestic legislation.

It is at this point that the relevancy of EC law in this dispute comes into play, in particular, Article 6 of the EC Habitats Directive 92/43[126], which imposes

---

[126] Council Directive 92/43/EEC of 21.5.1992 on the conservation of natural habitats and of wild fauna and flora, [1992] OJ L 206/7; see also the unofficial consolidated text of the Directive published in 2003, available at CELEX number: 392L0043. Art. 6 Habitats Directive reads as follows:

Article 6

1. For special areas of conservation, Member States shall establish the necessary conservation measures involving, if need be, appropriate management plans specifically designed for the sites or integrated into other development plans, and appropriate statutory, administrative or contractual measures which correspond to the ecological requirements of the natural habitat types in Annex I and the species in Annex II present on the sites.

2. Member States shall take appropriate steps to avoid, in the special areas of conservation, the deterioration of natural habitats and the habitats of species as well as disturbance of the species for which the areas have been designated, in so far as such disturbance could be significant in relation to the objectives of this Directive.

3. Any plan or project not directly connected with or necessary to the management of the site but likely to have a significant effect thereon, either individually or in combination with other plans or projects, shall be subject to appropriate assessment of its implications for the site in view of the site's conservation objectives. In the light of the conclusions of the assessment of the implications for the site and subject to the provisions of paragraph 4, the competent national authorities shall agree to the plan or project only after having ascertained that it will not adversely affect the integrity of the site concerned and, if appropriate, after having obtained the opinion of the general public.

4. If, in spite of a negative assessment of the implications for the site and in the absence of alternative solutions, a plan or project must nevertheless be carried out for imperative reasons of overriding public interest, including those of a social or economic nature, the Member State shall take all compensatory measures necessary to ensure that the overall coherence of Natura 2000 is protected. It shall inform the Commission of the compensatory measures adopted.

Where the site concerned hosts a priority natural habitat type and/or a priority species, the only considerations which may be raised are those relating to human health or public safety, to beneficial consequences of primary importance for the environment or, further to an opinion from the Commission, to other imperative reasons of overriding public interest.

See for recent cases concerning Article 6 Habitats Directive: Case C-418/04 *Commission v. Ireland* [2007]

strict conditions on any activities in a 'special area of conservation' such as the Meinweg area.

Despite the designation of protected status for the Meinweg area, Belgium expressed its intention of starting to use the railway line again. Accordingly, in the last decade discussions took place between Belgium and the Netherlands regarding its revitalisation. The environmental impact studies that were conducted determined that additional costs of about €500 million would be involved in order to meet the applicable environmental standards. Since no agreement was reached on who should pay the costs, both states agreed to solve the dispute by bringing it before an Arbitral Tribunal established under the auspices of the Permanent Court of Arbitration (PCA). In the *compromis* between the Netherlands and Belgium, the Arbitral Tribunal was explicitly called upon to settle the dispute on the basis of international law, including if necessary European law, while at the same time respecting the obligations of the parties arising out of Article 292 EC.

Although none of the parties challenged the jurisdiction of the Arbitral Tribunal, in its submission Belgium discussed the issue of Article 292 EC. It argued that even though both parties made references to EC law in their pleas, 'such references do not constitute sufficient reason to conclude that Article 292 EC had been violated'.[127] More specifically, Belgium distinguished the present dispute from the *MOX plant* case by arguing that 'unlike the UK in the *MOX plant* case, the Netherlands had not objected to Belgium's references to EC law in its Memorial.'[128]

Moreover, Belgium argued that neither party was contending that the other had violated EC law and that 'issues where Community law comes into play in the present case really boil down to the apportionment of costs, which is not a matter of Community law'.[129] Finally, it should be noted that both parties wrote a letter to the Secretary-General of the European Commission in which they stated that according to them the core of the dispute concerned the treaty of 1839. However, should the eventuality of an application or interpretation of Community law arise, both parties committed themselves to take all necessary measures in order to comply with Article 292 EC. In other words, both the Netherlands and Belgium essentially argued that EC law – including Article 292 EC – was not relevant to deciding the dispute.

Thus, whereas this dispute at first sight, and as presented by the parties, seemed to involve only international law aspects, the parties themselves recognized from the outset that European law, in particular Article 6 of the EC

ECR I-10947; Case C-508/04 *Commission v. Austria* [2007] ECR I-3787; Case C-388/05 *Commission v. Italy* [2007] ECR I-7555; Case C-239/04 *Commission v. Portugal* [2006] ECR I-10183; Case C-6/04 *Commission v. UK* [2005] ECR I-9017.

[127] Ad hoc Arbitral Tribunal, *IJzeren Rijn*, Arbitral Award, para. 13. See further: Warbrick (2007); Van Bladel (2005).

[128] *Ibid.*, para. 14.

[129] *Ibid.*

Habitats Directive, could potentially be relevant and thus expressly requested the arbitral tribunal to consider this issue as well.

3.2 The *IJzeren Rijn* Arbitral Tribunal Award

The *IJzeren Rijn* Arbitral Tribunal did indeed discuss three issues of Community law, namely, (i) Trans European Networks, (ii) Article 10 EC and (iii) the EC Habitats Directive. The following discussion is limited to the issue of the EC Habitats Directive, since this is the main issue and since the other two EC law aspects were treated in a similar way by the Arbitral Tribunal.

The Tribunal started its analysis concerning Article 292 EC by arguing that

> 'in regard to the limits drawn to its jurisdiction by Article 292 EC, it finds itself in a position analogous to that of a domestic court within the EC'.[130]

The Arbitral Tribunal continued by stating that if the tribunal arrived at the conclusion that it could not decide the case brought before it without engaging in the interpretation of EC laws which constitute neither *actes clairs* nor *actes éclairés* (i.e. the so-called *CILFIT* conditions), the obligation of Article 292 EC would be triggered and the dispute would have to be submitted to the ECJ.[131] Accordingly, the Arbitral Tribunal examined whether or not in the present case the *CILFIT* conditions were met.

The ECJ developed the *CILFIT* conditions in its jurisprudence concerning the obligation of national courts of the EC Member States to refer preliminary questions to it.[132] According to that jurisprudence, the obligation of national courts to refer preliminary questions to the ECJ is only waved (i) if the question is not relevant, (ii) if it has already been answered by the ECJ or (iii) if the answer is entirely clear so that there is no further need for the ECJ to give an answer.[133] It should be noted that the Arbitral Tribunal only examined the first possibility, i.e. whether the application of Community law was necessary for it to render an award in the dispute. The Arbitral Tribunal set out the framework of its jurisdiction by stating that

> 'from the viewpoint of Art. 292 EC the question thus faced by the Tribunal is [...] does the Tribunal have to engage in the interpretation of the Habitats Directive in

---

130 *Ibid.*, para. 103.

131 *Ibid.*

132 Case 283/81 *CILFIT* [1982] ECR 3415; as clarified in case C-244/01 *Köbler* [2003] ECR I-10239. But see the Opinion of AG Colomer in case C-461/03 *Gaston Schul* [2005] ECR I-10513. However, in its judgment the ECJ flatly rejected any relaxation of the *CILFIT* conditions as suggested by AG Colomer in C-461/03 *Gaston Schul* [2005] ECR I-10513.

133 See further: Chalmers (2006) 299-302; Steiner (2006) 210-217; Craig / De Búrca (2008) 460.

> order to enable it to decide the issue of the reactivation of the Iron Rhine railway and the costs involved?'[134]

After some discussion of the arguments of the parties, the Arbitral Tribunal turned its attention to the question of the legal basis on which the Meinweg area was designated a specially protected habitat area. According to the Arbitral Tribunal, this designation occurred in the first place on the basis of Dutch environmental legislation and not on that of the EC Habitats Directive. The Arbitral Tribunal then proceeded by determining first whether it had to interpret the EC Habitats Directive in order to render its award in the light of the *CILFIT* conditions. It concluded that:

> 'the Tribunal has examined whether it would arrive at different conclusions on the application of Art. XII to the Meinweg tunnel project and its costs if the Habitats Directive did not exist. The Tribunal answers this question in the negative, as its decision would be the same on the basis of Art. XII and of Netherlands environmental legislation alone. Hence the questions of EC law debated by the parties are not determinative, or conclusive for the Tribunal; it is not necessary for the Tribunal to interpret the Habitats Directive in order to render its award. Therefore, [...] the questions of EC law involved in the case do not trigger any obligations under Art. 292 EC.'[135]

As a result, the *IJzeren Rijn* Arbitral Tribunal considered itself able to render its award despite the fact that Community law (EC Habitats Directive and/or Article 292 EC) was clearly at issue and thus would have triggered the exclusive jurisdiction of the ECJ.

In substance, the *IJzeren Rijn* Arbitral Tribunal concluded that the Netherlands had to grant a right of transit to Belgium based on the Treaties of 1839 and 1897, but split the financial burden of the various parts of the reactivation project between both parties. Meanwhile, the responsible Dutch Minister of Transport has acknowledged that the IJzeren Rijn railway track will be reactivated if the search for other alternatives fails.[136] As far as the Dutch Government is concerned, the date of reactivation is currently envisaged as 2018.[137]

3.3 Commentary

It is remarkable that the *IJzeren Rijn* Arbitral Tribunal considered itself able to render its award despite the fact that Community law, i.e. the EC Habitats Directive, was clearly applicable in the dispute and thus needed

134 Ad hoc Arbitral Tribunal, *IJzeren Rijn*, Arbitral Award, para. 121, *op cit.*

135 *Ibid.*, para. 137.

136 See the letter of the responsible Dutch Minister to that effect of 25.11.2008, available at: http://www.verkeerenwaterstaat.nl/images/20082695_tcm195-233017.pdf.

137 *Ibid.*

to be applied and interpreted. This in turn would have triggered the exclusive jurisdiction of the ECJ based on Article 292 EC.

Nonetheless, the *IJzeren Rijn* Arbitral Tribunal not only exercised its jurisdiction, but did so without taking the EC Habitats Directive or the relevant ECJ jurisprudence into account at all, whereas it was clearly applicable. Moreover, due to the fact that the *IJzeren Rijn* Arbitral Tribunal was from the outset not in a position to request a preliminary ruling from the ECJ because it did not meet the conditions of a proper court within the meaning of Article 234 EC[138], it was all the more obliged to refuse its jurisdiction in this case and refer the parties to the ECJ as the only proper forum. Accordingly, it undermined the uniform application of Community law in all EC Member States.

It is indeed interesting to note that the ECJ seems to have been powerless to prevent EC Member States from bringing a dispute which clearly ought to have been brought before it before another international court or tribunal. Above all, it is remarkable that the Member States got away with it. Unlike in the *MOX plant* dispute, the European Commission was not inclined to take up the case in order to protect Article 292 EC.

Moreover, the *IJzeren Rijn* award proves the ECJ right that the uniformity and consistency of Community law can be undermined by the proliferation of international courts and tribunals, and more importantly, if these international courts and tribunals fail to take relevant Community law and ECJ jurisprudence into account.

At the same time, however, this case may also be seen as an indication of the increasing need of EC Member States to be able to use other dispute settlement fora than the ECJ. Clearly, there are some advantages which induce Member States to prefer to choose an ad hoc arbitral tribunal rather the ECJ, such as

---

[138] In case C-125/04 *Denuit and Cordenier v. Transorient* [2005] ECR I-923, the ECJ formulated the conditions for a court or tribunal to be able to request a preliminary ruling from the ECJ as follows:
'12. In order to determine whether a body making a reference is a court or tribunal of a Member State for the purposes of Article 234 EC, the Court takes account of a number of factors, such as whether the body is established by law, whether it is permanent, whether its jurisdiction is compulsory, whether its procedure is *inter partes*, whether it applies rules of law and whether it is independent (see, in particular, Case C-54/96 *Dorsch Consult* [1997] ECR I-4961, paragraph 23, and the case-law there cited, and Case C-516/99 *Schmid* [2002] ECR I-4573, paragraph 34).
13. Under the Court's case-law, an arbitration tribunal is not a court or tribunal of a Member State' within the meaning of Article 234 EC where the parties are under no obligation, in law or in fact, to refer their disputes to arbitration and the public authorities of the Member State concerned are not involved in the decision to opt for arbitration nor required to intervene of their own accord in the proceedings before the arbitrator (Case 102/81 *Nordsee Deutsche Hochseefischerei* [1982] ECR 1095, paragraphs 10 to 12, and Case C-126/97 *Eco Swiss* [1999] ECR I-3055, paragraph 34).' It is submitted that this also applies in analogy to international arbitral tribunals.

faster proceedings, the selection of arbitrators, the determination of the rules of procedure, and confidentiality.[139]

Nonetheless, from the point of view of preserving the unity and consistency of law, the preferred option is that courts and arbitral tribunals interpret and apply relevant EC law provisions in the light of existing ECJ jurisprudence. In this way, courts and tribunals are able to exercise their jurisdiction, while at the same time ensuring consistency between the international and Community law obligations of the EC Member States involved in a dispute.

4 The *Mexican soft drinks* dispute

4.1 The factual and legal background

In 2004 the US complained about certain tax measures imposed by Mexico on soft drinks and other beverages that use any sweetener other than cane sugar. The tax measures concerned included: (i) a 20% tax on soft drinks and other beverages that use any sweetener other than cane sugar ('beverage tax'), which is not applied to beverages that use cane sugar; and (ii) a 20% tax on the commissioning, mediation, agency, representation, brokerage, consignment and distribution of soft drinks and other beverages that use any sweetener other than cane sugar ('distribution tax').

The US considered these taxes to be inconsistent with Article III of GATT 1994, in particular with Article III:2, first and second sentences, and Article III:4 thereof. Accordingly, the US requested consultations with Mexico, which ended unsuccessfully. As a consequence, the US instituted dispute settlement proceedings before the WTO against Mexico.[140]

As a preliminary point, Mexico raised the issue of jurisdictional competition. More specifically, it requested the WTO panel to decide to decline to exercise its jurisdiction in favour of an Arbitral Panel under Chapter Twenty of the North American Free Trade Agreement (NAFTA).[141] In short, Mexico argued that this dispute involved two NAFTA states and touched on NAFTA provisions and therefore should be treated as a NAFTA dispute rather than a WTO dispute. Indeed, Mexico claimed that it had adopted the measure in order to force the US to cooperate in finding a resolution to the dispute within the framework of NAFTA. Accordingly, Mexico argued, a NAFTA panel would be in a better position to decide. In this context it should be noted that Mexico and the U.S. have for quite some time been involved in a broader dispute on sugar, which has been litigated in various proceedings before the WTO and NAFTA.[142]

---

139 Malintoppi (2006).

140 WTO Panel Report, *Mexico-Tax measures on soft drinks and other beverages*, WT/DS308/R, 7.10.2005.

141 *Ibid.*, para. 7.1.

142 For a detailed discussion see: Davey / Sapir (2009); Vacek-Aranda (2006); Larios (2005).

4.2 The WTO Panel and Appellate Body rulings

4.2.1 The WTO Panel ruling

In a preliminary ruling, the WTO panel rejected Mexico's request and found instead that under the WTO Dispute Settlement Understanding (DSU) it had no discretion to decide whether or not to exercise its jurisdiction in a case properly put before it.[143] The WTO panel added that even if it had such discretion, it 'did not consider that there were facts on record that would justify the panel declining to exercise its jurisdiction in the present case.'[144]

In its reasoning, the WTO panel opined that 'discretion may be said to exist only if a legal body has the freedom to choose among several options, all of them equally permissible in law.'[145] According to the panel,

> 'such freedom [...] would exist within the framework of the DSU only if a complainant did not have a legal right to have a panel decide a case properly before it.'[146]

Referring to Article 11 of the DSU and to the ruling of the Appellate Body in *Australia – Salmon*, the panel observed that the aim of the WTO dispute settlement system is to resolve the matter at issue in particular cases and to secure a positive solution to disputes, and that a panel is required to address the claims on which a finding is necessary to enable the Dispute Settlement Body (DSB) to make sufficiently precise recommendations or rulings to the parties.[147] From this, the panel concluded that a WTO panel would not therefore seem to be in a position to choose freely whether or not to exercise its jurisdiction.[148] Referring to Articles 3.2 and 19.2 of the DSU, the panel further stated that if a WTO panel were to decide not to exercise its jurisdiction in a particular case, it would diminish the rights of the complaining Member under the DSU and other WTO-covered agreements.[149] The WTO panel added that Article 23 of the DSU makes it clear that a WTO Member that considers that any of its WTO benefits have been nullified or impaired as a result of a measure adopted by another Member has the right to bring the case before the WTO dispute settlement system.[150]

Finally, regarding the potential jurisdictional competition between the NAFTA and WTO dispute settlement systems, it should be noted that the WTO panel did not make any findings on whether there may be other cases where

---

[143] *Supra* note 140, Annex B, Fax of the Chairman of the Panel, dated 18 January 2005.

[144] *Ibid.*

[145] *Ibid.*, para. 7.7.

[146] *Ibid.*

[147] *Ibid.*, para. 7.8, referring to WTO Appellate Body Report, *Australia – Measures affecting importation of Salmon*, WT/DS18/AB/R, 20.10.1998, para. 223.

[148] *Ibid.*

[149] *Ibid.*, para. 7.9.

[150] *Ibid.*

a WTO panel's jurisdiction might be legally constrained, notwithstanding its approved terms of reference.[151] In any case, the WTO panel explicitly rejected Mexico's contention that this WTO proceeding was identical with the on-going negotiations to resolve the sugar dispute within the NAFTA context.[152] Consequently, the WTO panel concluded that

> '[...] even conceding that there seems to be an unresolved dispute between Mexico and the United States under the NAFTA, the resolution of the present WTO case cannot be linked to the NAFTA dispute. In turn, any findings made by this panel, as well as its conclusions and recommendations in the present case, only relate to Mexico's rights and obligations under the WTO-covered agreements, and not to its rights and obligations under other international agreements, such as the NAFTA, or other rules of international law.'[153]

4.2.2 The WTO Appellate Body ruling

On appeal before the WTO Appellate Body, Mexico argued that the panel erred in rejecting its request that it decline to exercise jurisdiction in the circumstances of the present dispute.[154] Mexico submitted that WTO panels, like other international bodies and tribunals, have certain implied jurisdictional powers that derive from their nature as adjudicative bodies. Such powers include the power to refrain from exercising substantive jurisdiction in circumstances where the underlying or predominant elements of a dispute derive from rules of international law under which claims cannot be judicially enforced in the WTO, such as the NAFTA provisions, or when one of the disputing parties refuses to take the matter to the appropriate forum. Mexico argued, in this regard, that the American claims under Article III of the GATT 1994 are inextricably linked to a broader dispute regarding the access of Mexican sugar to the US market under the NAFTA. Mexico further emphasized that there is nothing in the DSU that explicitly rules out the existence of a WTO panel's power to decline to exercise validly-established jurisdiction. Accordingly, Mexico argued that the WTO panel should have exercised this power in the circumstances of this dispute. In

---

151 *Ibid.*, para. 7.10.

152 *Ibid.*, para. 7.14. The Panel noted, in this regard, that:

'In the present case, the complaining party is the United States and the measures in dispute are allegedly imposed by Mexico. In the NAFTA case, the situation appears to be the reverse: the complaining party is Mexico and the measures in dispute are allegedly imposed by the United States. As for the subject matter of the claims, in the present case the United States is alleging discriminatory treatment against its products resulting from internal taxes and other internal measures imposed by Mexico. In the NAFTA case, instead, Mexico is arguing that the United States is violating its market access commitments under the NAFTA.'

153 *Ibid.*, para. 7.15.

154 WTO Appellate Body report, *Mexico – Tax measures on soft drinks and other beverages*, WT/DS308/AB/R, 6.3.2006. See generally: Jimenez (2006).

contrast, the US argued that the WTO panel's own terms of reference in this dispute instructed the panel to examine the matter referred to the DSB by the US and to make such findings as will assist the DSB in making the recommendations and rulings provided for under the DSU.

The WTO Appellate Body started its analysis by noting that Mexico did not question whether the WTO panel had jurisdiction to hear the American claims. Moreover, Mexico did not claim that there were legal obligations under NAFTA, or any other international agreement to which Mexico and the US are both parties, which might raise legal impediments to the panel hearing this case. Instead, Mexico's position was that, although the WTO panel had the authority to rule on the merits of the American claims, it also had the 'implied power' to abstain from ruling on them, and should have exercised this power in the circumstances of this dispute. Hence, the issue before the Appellate Body was not whether the WTO panel was legally precluded from ruling on the American claims that were before it, but rather whether the WTO panel could have, and should have, declined, to exercise jurisdiction with respect to the American claims under Article III of the GATT 1994 that were before it.

The WTO Appellate Body continued by agreeing with Mexico's claim that WTO panels have certain powers that are inherent in their adjudicative function. Notably, WTO panels have the right to determine whether they have jurisdiction in a given case, as well as to determine the scope of their jurisdiction. In this regard, the WTO Appellate Body had previously stated that

> 'it is a widely accepted rule that an international tribunal is entitled to consider the issue of its own jurisdiction on its own initiative, and to satisfy itself that it has jurisdiction in any case that comes before it.'[155]

Furthermore, the WTO Appellate Body had also explained that WTO panels have 'a margin of discretion to deal, always in accordance with due process, with specific situations that may arise in a particular case and that are not explicitly regulated.'[156] For example, WTO panels may exercise judicial economy; that is, refrain from ruling on certain claims when such rulings are not necessary to resolve the matter at issue in a dispute.[157] However, at the same time the WTO

---

[155] WTO Appellate Body Report, *US – Anti-Dumping Act of 1916*, WT/DS136/AB/R and WT/DS162/AB/R, 28 August 2000, footnote 30 to para. 54. See also WTO Appellate Body Report, *Mexico – Corn Syrup* (Article 21.5 – US), WT/DS132/AB/RW, 22 October 2001, para. 36: '[...] panels have to address and dispose of certain issues of a fundamental nature, even if the parties to the dispute remain silent on those issues. ... [P]anels cannot simply ignore issues which go to the root of their jurisdiction—that is, to their authority to deal with and dispose of matters. Rather, panels must deal with such issues—if necessary, on their own motion—in order to satisfy themselves that they have authority to proceed'.

[156] WTO Appellate Body Report, *EC – Hormones*, WT/DS48/AB/R, 16.1.1998, footnote 138 to para. 152. See also WTO Appellate Body Report, *US – FSC* (Article 21.5 – EC), WT/DS108/AB/RW, 14.1.2002, paras. 247-248.

[157] WTO Appellate Body Report, *US – Wool Shirts and Blouses*, WT/DS33/AB/R, 23.5.1997, para. 340.

Appellate Body had cautioned that to provide only a partial resolution of the matter at issue would be a false judicial economy.[158]

In the WTO Appellate Body's view, it does not necessarily follow, however, from the existence of these inherent adjudicative powers that, once jurisdiction has been validly established, WTO panels would have the authority to decline to rule on the entirety of the claims that are before them in a dispute. On the contrary, the WTO Appellate Body noted that while recognizing WTO panels' inherent powers it had previously emphasized that:

> 'Although panels enjoy some discretion in establishing their own working procedures, *this discretion does not extend to modifying the substantive provisions of the DSU.* [...] *Nothing in the DSU gives a panel the authority either to disregard or to modify [...] explicit provisions of the DSU.*'[159] [emphasis added]

Indeed, the fact that a WTO member may initiate a WTO dispute whenever it considers that any benefits accruing to it are being impaired by measures taken by another member implies that that member is *entitled* to a ruling by a WTO panel. According to the WTO Appellate Body, a decision by a WTO panel to decline to exercise validly established jurisdiction would seem to diminish the right of a complaining member to seek the redress of a violation of obligations within the meaning of Article 23 of the DSU, and to bring a dispute pursuant to Article 3.3 of the DSU. This would not be consistent with a panel's obligations under Articles 3.2 and 19.2 of the DSU.[160]

Finally, regarding the issue of jurisdictional competition the WTO Appellate Body, like the WTO panel, did not express a view as to whether there may be other circumstances in which legal impediments could exist that would preclude a panel from ruling on the merits of the claims that are before it. Thus, the WTO Appellate Body saw no reason to disagree with the panel's decision.

As regards the substance of the sugar dispute between Mexico and the US, it should be noted that Mexico implemented the WTO Appellate Body ruling and subsequently reached an agreement with the U.S. on the supply of sugar and other sweeteners.[161]

---

[158] WTO Appellate Body Report, *Australia – Measures affecting importation of Salmon, op cit.*, para. 223.

[159] WTO Appellate Body Report, *India – Patents (U.S.)*, WT/DS50/AB/R, 19.12.1997, para. 92.

[160] Article 3.2 of the DSU provides that 'recommendations and rulings of the DSB cannot add to or diminish the rights and obligations provided in the covered agreements.' Article 19.2 of the DSU states that 'in accordance with paragraph 2 of Article 3, in their findings and recommendations, the panel and Appellate Body cannot add to or diminish the rights and obligations provided in the covered agreements.'

[161] See: Kornis (2008).

4.3 Commentary

Although, the WTO panel and Appellate Body were able to avoid dealing with the issue of jurisdictional competition mainly on factual grounds, the *Mexico soft drinks*[162] case illustrates the general attitude and approach of the WTO Appellate Body on this issue.

The WTO Appellate Body seems to argue that if a WTO panel has jurisdiction in a case, it must exercise it by rendering a ruling, regardless of whether or not other courts or tribunals might have jurisdiction or have been involved with the dispute. Of course, a different approach is clearly imaginable in which a WTO panel or Appellate Body relinquishes its jurisdiction and orders the parties to resolve their dispute before the other dispute settlement body, or alternatively the WTO panel or Appellate Body could stay the proceedings until that other body rendered its decision. In this way, the WTO panel or Appellate Body could then take that decision into account when adjudicating the dispute.

Like the ECJ in the *MOX plant* case, the WTO Appellate Body shows little comity towards other international courts and tribunals that may be equally or even better suited to deal with the dispute. It is submitted that this attitude is not very helpful in view of the fact that more cases raising the jurisdictional competition issue in the WTO-RTA nexus must be expected in the future.[163] Indeed, the next case study is a good example of this development.

5 The *Brazilian Tyres* dispute

5.1 The factual and legal background

One of the most serious yet common diseases in Brazil is dengue fever. It is transmitted by a certain species of mosquito (*Aedes aegypti*), which is found in tropical and subtropical countries. It breeds in stagnant water found, amongst other places, in the 100 million waste tyres scattered throughout the country. There is no specific treatment for dengue fever or vaccine available to prevent it, and it can be fatal. Dengue is a problem that has affected Brazil since the 19th Century and is believed to have originated in the State of Rio de Janeiro. The last three national outbreaks were in 1986, 1991 and 2001 and during them more than two million cases were reported.[164] To combat the

[162] It should be noted that in the meantime Mexico has modified the relevant national provisions in order to implement the WTO Appellate Body report, see: Status Report by Mexico, *Mexico – Tax measures on soft drinks and other beverages*, WT/DS308/16, 12.1.2007. As a result, the US withdrew the Art. 21 (3) DSU procedure it had initiated. See: Agreement under Article 21.3(b) of the DSU, *Mexico – Tax measures on soft drinks and other beverages*, WT/DS308/15, 5.7.2006.

[163] See generally: Henckels (2008); Gao / Lim (2008); Hassanien (2008).

[164] Figueiredo (2003) 25. It should be noted that the dengue problem has become so widespread that a Second International Conference on Dengue and Dengue Haemorrhagic Fever was organised in Octo-

problem of Brazil's continuous health crisis caused by deadly tropical mosquitoes, its legislative and executive branches decided to pass as many measures as possible.

The Brazilian government therefore found it necessary as long ago as 1991 to dramatically curb the import of breeding sites for the *Aedes* mosquito, the most popular and widespread being used tyres. Retreaded tyres were also, albeit inexplicitly and controversially, included in this import ban until 2000, when the law was consolidated for clarity. At this time the legislation went under scrutiny not only in Brazilian courts but also in the MERCOSUR and WTO dispute settlement bodies.[165]

The first piece of legislation was Ministerial Act Portaria DECEX 9/1991, which prohibited the importation of used tyres. As previously stated, retreaded tyres would often also non-expressly fall into this category. In 1996 Brazil enacted CONAMA 23/1996 in order to reduce non-disposed tyre waste. This resolution established that inert waste is free from import restrictions with the exception of used tyres.

In 2000 Brazil explicitly banned the importation of retreaded (and used) tyres in its territory by means of Portaria SECEX 8/2000. Following the adoption of this legislation, Uruguay requested the initiation of arbitral proceedings within MERCOSUR in August 2001, claiming that the import ban violated its right to free trade as guaranteed by the MERCUROS treaty.

5.2 The various judicial decisions on the *Brazilian Tyres* dispute

5.2.1 The MERCOSUR ad hoc Arbitral Tribunal Award

The MERCOSUR ad hoc Arbitral Tribunal started its analysis by acknowledging that there had been an important, continuous and growing commercial influx of remoulded tyres from Uruguay to Brazil in the 1990's, during the time of Portaria DECEX 8/1991.[166] Moreover, following the perusal of several documents from different organs and authorities of the Brazilian government, it concluded that Portaria SECEX 8/2000 did in fact modify the import ban to include retreaded tyres, and hence did not merely clarify DECEX 8/1991. This modification affected the practice of State agencies, as a result of which remoulded tyres from Uruguay were no longer being given access to the Brazilian market as guaranteed by the MERCOSUR.

The Arbitral Tribunal also found that although Resolution 109/94 of the Common Market Group grants member states the independence to legislate on the import of used goods, one must take into account Decision no. 22/2000, also of the Common Market Group. The latter legislation, and in particular the

ber 2008 in Phuket, Thailand, available at: http://www.dengue2008phuket.com/conference/index.php.

165 See for a detailed analysis: Lavranos / Vielliard (2008d).

166 MERCOSUR ad hoc Arbitral Tribunal, *Uruguay v. Brazil (Remoulded Tyres)*, 9.1.2002.

date it came into force, is crucial in the assessment of Portaria SECEX 8/2000. It prohibits *new inter se* restrictions of trade, and as it came into force prior to Portaria SECEX 8/2000, Brazil could not introduce new restrictions which affected the trade in remoulded tyres.

Finally, the Tribunal found that irrespective of its compatibility with Decision no. 22/2000, Portaria SECEX 8/2000 was contrary to the principle of estoppel, since Uruguay's uninterrupted export of remoulded tyres while Portaria DECEX 8/1991 was in force was cut short by the 2000 Brazilian legislation. In the Tribunal's view, such a sudden change of attitude went against the spirit of integration of the MERCOSUR.[167]

In sum, Brazil's clarification of its legislation by explicitly banning the import of retreaded tyres, although defensible, was considered by the MERCOSUR *ad hoc* Arbitral Tribunal to be inconsistent with Brazil's existing MERCOSUR trade law obligations. Since at the time of this ruling the Protocol of Olivos was still being drafted[168], Brazil had no right of appeal. Consequently, Brazil had no choice but to adopt new legislation in order to comply with the MERCOSUR Arbitral Tribunal's ruling.

5.2.2 The WTO Panel ruling

As a result of the MERCOSUR ad hoc Arbitral Tribunal's award, Brazil amended its legislation to comply with its findings. Accordingly, Brazil enacted Portaria SECEX 2/2002, which eliminated the import ban for remoulded tyres (a particular kind of retreaded tyres) originating in other MERCOSUR countries. This exemption was incorporated into Article 40 of Portaria SECEX 14/2004, which contains three main elements: (i) an import ban on retreaded tyres (the 'import ban'); (ii) an import ban on used tyres; and (iii) an exemption from the import ban on remoulded tyres from other countries of the MERCOSUR, which is referred to as the 'MERCOSUR exemption'. In this context, it must be emphasised that the 'MERCOSUR exemption' did not form part of previous regulations prohibiting the importation of retreaded tyres, notably Portaria SECEX 8/2000, but was introduced in order to implement the MERCOSUR *ad hoc* Arbitral Tribunal's award.

It was Portaria SECEX 14/2004 which prompted the EC to bring this dispute before the WTO, contesting the conformity of Brazil's import ban and the 'MERCOSUR exemption' with WTO law. Consequently, the EC made a request for consultations with Brazil in June 2005. Failing a mutually acceptable agree-

---

[167] *Ibid.*

[168] The Protocol of Olivios, which entered into force on 1 January 2004, among other things established a MERCOSUR Permanent Review Court consisting of 5 arbitrators. For a detailed analysis see: Pisctiello / Schmidt (2007); Vinuesa (2006).

ment, the matter progressed to the establishment of a WTO Panel and thereafter to an appeal by the EC to the WTO Appellate Body.[169]

The WTO Panel accepted that the 'MERCOSUR exemption' was not motivated by 'capricious or unpredictable reasons'[170], but merely resulted from a decision by the MERCOSUR ad hoc Arbitral Tribunal adjudicating a dispute amongst MERCOSUR members on the basis of MERCOSUR law, the results of which were legally binding on Brazil. It then went further in noting that Article XXIV GATT provides for preferential treatment to members of an agreement intended to liberalise trade such as a customs union, to the detriment of other countries.[171] In its view, even though it did not pronounce the MERCOSUR as legally qualifying as a Customs Union in accordance with the GATT, discrimination between members of the MERCOSUR and members of the WTO under the umbrella of Article XXIV GATT was not *a priori* unreasonable.[172]

The WTO Panel continued its analysis by turning to the argument raised by the EC, namely that Brazil had failed to rely on Article 50 (d) of the Treaty of Montevideo[173], which serves a similar function as Article XX GATT, before the MERCOSUR Arbitral Tribunal. Essentially, the EC argued that due to this failure Brazil was no longer entitled to rely on the Article XX GATT exception in the WTO proceedings.

However, the WTO Panel had chosen not to discuss this issue.[174] In fact, it explicitly stated that it was not in a position to assess in detail the choice of arguments by Brazil in the MERCOSUR proceedings or to second-guess the outcome of the case in the light of Brazil's litigation strategy in those proceedings.[175] Indeed, the Panel considered it inappropriate to engage in such an exercise.[176] Moreover, it underlined that while the particular litigation strategy followed in that instance by Brazil turned out to be unsuccessful, it was not clear that a different strategy would necessarily have led to a different outcome.[177] The WTO

---

[169] WTO Panel Report, *Brazil – Measures Affecting Imports of Retreaded Tyres*, WT/DS332/R, 12.6.2007; WTO Appellate Body Report, *Brazil – Measures Affecting Imports of Retreaded Tyres*, WT/DS332/AB/R, 3.12.2007.

[170] WTO Panel Report, *Brazil – Measures Affecting Imports of Retreaded Tyres*, at para. 7.272.

[171] *Ibid.* See for an interesting analysis: Pauwelyn (2007).

[172] *Ibid.*, paras. 7.273, 7.274.

[173] Treaty of Montevideo, Instrument Establishing the Latin American Integration Association (ALADI), signed in Montevideo, August 1980. Article 50(d) reads as follows:

'No provision under the present Treaty shall be interpreted as precluding the adoption and observance of measures regarding:

[...]

d. Protection of human, animal and plant life and health.'

[174] WTO Panel Report, *Brazil – Measures Affecting Imports of Retreaded Tyres*, para. 7.275.

[175] *Ibid.*, para. 7.276.

[176] *Ibid.*

[177] *Ibid.*

Panel simply stated that Brazil's litigation strategy did not seem 'unreasonable or absurd'.[178]

In substance, the WTO Panel found that Brazil's measures were not justified under Article XX GATT. This was notwithstanding the Panel's conclusion that Brazil had demonstrated that the alternative measures identified by the EC (i.e. land filling, stockpiling, incineration and recycling) did not constitute reasonably available alternatives to the import ban on retreaded tyres that would achieve Brazil's objective of reducing the accumulation of waste tyres on its territory, and therefore that Brazil's import ban could be considered 'necessary' within the meaning of Article XX (b) GATT. In effect, Brazil's defence under Article XX GATT failed at the chapeau level.[179] Having adjudicated on the above, the Panel decided to exercise judicial economy regarding Brazil's defence that the 'MERCOSUR exemption' was justified under Article XXIV GATT.

In sum, although Brazil failed in its Article XX GATT defence and hence substantially lost the case, the WTO Panel did not make any negative findings against the 'MERCOSUR exemption', which was the main aim of the EC in bringing the case. On the contrary, it was the only measure which complied with the chapeau of Article XX GATT. Had Brazil had a better grip on the enforcement of the import ban, the Panel may well have got it off the hook.[180]

5.2.3 The WTO Appellate Body ruling

In contrast to the WTO Panel, the WTO Appellate Body picked up the EC's argument and noted that Brazil could have sought to justify the challenged import ban on the grounds of human, animal, and plant health under Article 50(d) of the Treaty of Montevideo. As mentioned above, Brazil decided not to do so. Although, the Appellate Body explicitly stated that it would not be appropriate for it to second-guess Brazil's decision not to invoke Article 50(d), in reality the WTO Appellate Body discussed Brazil's defence strategy before the MERCOSUR Arbitral Tribunal. Indeed, the WTO Appellate Body inferred from Brazil's failure to invoke Article 50 (d) of the Treaty of Montevideo as a defence in the MERCOSUR arbitral proceedings that the discrimination associated with the 'MERCOSUR exemption' does not necessarily result from a conflict between provisions under MERCOSUR and the GATT.[181]

In substance, like the Panel, the Appellate Body found that the import ban was necessary to achieve Brazil's objective in accordance with Article XX (b)

---

[178] *Ibid.*

[179] The chapeau of Article XX of the GATT reads as follows: 'subject to the requirement that such measures are not applied in a manner which would constitute a means of arbitrary or unjustifiable discrimination between countries, where the same conditions prevail, or a disguised restriction on international trade, nothing in this Agreement shall be construed to prevent the adoption or enforcement by any contracting party of measures: (a)-(j)'.

[180] Van Calster (2007).

[181] WTO Appellate Body Report, *Brazil – Measures Affecting Imports of Retreaded Tyres*, para. 234.

GATT. It also sided with the Panel in finding that Brazil's decision to act in order to comply with the MERCOSUR Arbitral Tribunal's ruling could not be viewed as 'capricious' or 'random'.[182] However, it added that discrimination can result from a rational decision or behaviour and still be 'arbitrary' or 'unjustifiable' because it is explained by a rationale that bears no relationship to the objective of a measure provisionally justified under Article XX GATT, or goes against that objective. In the Appellate Body's view, the MERCOSUR *ad hoc* Arbitral Tribunal's decision was not an acceptable rationale for discrimination against imports from the EC, because it bore no relationship to the legitimate objective to be achieved by the import ban, and actually went against it.[183]

The Appellate Body further reiterated that the function of the chapeau is the prevention of abuse of the exceptions specified in the paragraphs of Article XX GATT.[184] It therefore concluded that the 'MERCOSUR exemption' had resulted in the import ban being applied in a manner that constituted arbitrary or unjustifiable discrimination.[185] In the same light and consequently, the WTO Appellate Body also found, contrary to the Panel, that the 'MERCOSUR exemption' was applied in a manner that constituted a disguised restriction on international trade.[186]

In sum, the WTO Appellate Body reversed the Panel's application of the chapeau of Article XX GATT by rejecting its quantitative analysis and instead looking into the cause of the discrimination or the rationale put forward to explain its existence.[187] In doing so, it found that the 'MERCOSUR exemption' did infringe the chapeau of Article XX GATT.[188]

5.3 Commentary

The *Brazilian Tyres* case can be considered an evolution from the *Mexican soft drinks* case, as the WTO Panel and Appellate Body could, but did not, circumvent the issue of competing jurisdiction caused by the MERCOSUR Arbitral Tribunal's ruling. This dispute is interesting in particular because it shows the divergent approach adopted by the WTO Panel and the Appellate Body regarding the level of deference that should be accorded to the MERCOSUR Arbitral Tribunal's ruling.

It is submitted that the WTO Panel was correct in not reviewing or criticising the ruling of the MERCOSUR Arbitral Tribunal, but rather accepted it as a fact and the starting point of the whole dispute. Similarly, the WTO Panel quite

---

[182] *Ibid.*, para. 232.

[183] *Ibid.*, para. 228.

[184] *Ibid.*, para. 224. See also: WTO Appellate Body Report, *US – Standards for Reformulated and Conventional Gasoline*, WT/DS2/AB/R, 20.5.1996.

[185] *Ibid.*, para. 228.

[186] *Ibid.*, para. 239.

[187] See further: Van Calster (2008).

[188] For a critical analysis of the Appellate Body conclusions see: Brown / Trachtman (2009).

rightly refrained from assessing Brazil's defence strategy before the MERCOSUR Arbitral Tribunal. Indeed, it is argued that the defence strategy of a WTO member before another dispute settlement body, which is not bound by WTO law, is entirely its own business and that any assessment of it by WTO Panels or the WTO Appellate Body would go far beyond their competence. This applies equally to the reviewing of the MERCOSUR Arbitral Tribunal's ruling by the WTO Appellate Body or WTO Panels.

In this context it should be noted that in a very similar subsequent dispute between Uruguay and Argentina, also concerning an import ban on retreaded tyres, the MERCOSUR Permanent Review Court rejected Argentina's defence under Article 50 (d) of the Montevideo Treaty stating that the principle of utmost importance in an integration system such as the MERCOSUR is free trade.[189] Thus, even if Brazil had raised the Article 50 (d) defence in the MERCOSUR proceedings it most probably would have lost the case.

The fact that the WTO Appellate Body engaged in such a review exhibits a sort of supremacy which the WTO Appellate Body is attaching to WTO law over other regional trade agreements or indeed decisions rendered by dispute settlement bodies that have been established by such treaties. In other words, it seems that the WTO Appellate Body is suggesting that other dispute settlement bodies must issue their decisions in conformity with WTO law and Appellate Body jurisprudence, or otherwise face the possibility of being reviewed and revised by the WTO Appellate Body.

This attitude is also visible in the most recent WTO decision under Article 21.3 (c) DSU in this dispute.[190] Here, the Arbitrator also discussed the possibility of raising the Article 50 (d) of the Treaty of Montevideo defence in the light of the decision of the MERCOSUR Permanent Review Court in the *Uruguay v. Argentina* dispute mentioned above. The Arbitrator opined that, while it was not his task as arbitrator to discuss the substance of the dispute as determined by the WTO panel and Appellate Body[191], he rightly considered the ruling in the *Uruguay v. Argentina* case not binding on Brazil.[192] Nonetheless, the Arbitrator found it necessary to discuss the issue of Article 50 (d) Montevideo Treaty further. According to the Arbitrator, even though Argentina's reliance on this article was unsuccessful because of the disproportionate nature of Argentina's measures, the invocation of Article 50 (d) was – in the view of the Arbitrator – not excluded in principle by the MERCOSUR Permanent Review Court.[193]

The Arbitrator went even further in his review of the MERCOSUR Arbitral Tribunal's ruling by remarking that its ruling

---

[189] Mercosur Ad hoc Arbitral Tribunal, *Uruguay v. Argentina – Import prohibition of remoulded tyres from Uruguay*, 25.10.2005; subsequently overturned on appeal by the Mercosur Permanent Review Court, *Uruguay v Argentina – Import prohibition of remoulded tyres from Uruguay*, 22.12.2005.

[190] Award of the Arbitrator, *Brazil – Measures Affecting Imports of Retreaded Tyres*, WT/DS332/16, 29.8.2008.

[191] *Ibid.*, para. 82.

[192] *Ibid.*, para. 82, explanation in footnote 141.

[193] *Ibid.*

'[...] does not, and did not need to, reflect and interpret all rights and obligations under MERCOSUR law that are relevant to the manner in which Brazil may choose to implement the DSB recommendations and rulings'.[194]

It seems as if the WTO Arbitrator was suggesting that the MERCOSUR ad hoc Arbitral Tribunal did not properly and fully understand and apply MERCOSUR law in its *Brazilian Tyres* decision. Obviously, the question arises of whether a WTO Arbitrator is in a position to openly challenge and criticize the decision of another tribunal that has been established under another trade regime, and even more so of whether this is appropriate in terms of comity and judicial respect.

It is submitted that the assessment of Brazil's defence strategy by the WTO Appellate Body was an unprecedented interference in Brazil's sovereignty in defending its interests before another dispute settlement body that is fully independent and free from any 'supervision' by the WTO Appellate Body. Indeed, there is no WTO supremacy over dispute settlement bodies established by regional trade agreements.

However, the *Brazilian Tyres* case seems to illustrate that there is a shift – at least from the point of view of the WTO Appellate Body – from a horizontal relationship between the WTO and a RTA such as the MERCOSUR towards a vertical relationship by seeming to put the WTO legal order at the very top.

In sum, the different approaches of the WTO Panel and Appellate Body on this point unveil the underlying potential problems of competing jurisdiction between dispute settlement systems created by regional trade agreements (like NAFTA and MERCOSUR) and the global WTO dispute settlement system.[195] In view of the increasing number of dispute settlement systems being established and developed at the regional level[196], it is doubtful whether the WTO Appellate Body's claim of supremacy over other dispute settlement bodies is the most co-operative answer to this problem. [197]

---

194 *Ibid.*

195 See generally: Gama Sá Cabral / Lucarelli de Salvio (2008); Leal-Arcas (2007); Tiny (2005); Davey (2006); Hsu (2006); Van Damme (2006).

196 See the recent developments regarding the dispute settlement system of MERCOSUR: Pavon / Schmidt (2007); Appleton / Graf (2007). See regarding the SADC: Pauwelyn (2004). See concerning the SAFTA: Nath (2007). See regarding Central America: Gantz (2007).

197 Tiny, *supra* note 195. See also: WTO Panel Report, *Turkey – Restrictions on Imports of Textile and Clothing Products*, WT/DS34/R, 31.5.1999; WTO Appellate Body Report, *Turkey – Restrictions on Imports of Textile and Clothing Products*, WT/DS34/AB/R, 22.10.1999.

6 The ICTY's *Tadic* test v. the ICJ's *Nicaragua* test

6.1 The factual and legal background

The war and killings in the Balkans were so widespread that a special court – the International Criminal Tribunal for the former Yugoslavia (ICTY) – was established by the UN so as to hold individuals responsible for those acts.[198] Accordingly, the ICTY has rendered numerous judgments in which it has punished individuals responsible for the horrendous crimes, such as ethnic cleansing and mass rapes that were committed in the 1990s.[199]

In one of the most discussed cases, *Tadic*[200], the ICTY had to determine whether or not Tadic's individual responsibility could be established. In order to determine that, the ICTY first had to establish whether or not the conditions for state responsibility of the Former Republic of Yugoslavia (FRY), under which Tadic supposedly committed the crimes, were met. To answer this question, the ICTY had to examine one of the main elements of state responsibility, namely, the degree to which the FRY exercised control over Tadic. The ICTY Chamber identified two degrees of control: the ICJ's *Nicaragua*[201] 'effective control' test and the 'overall control' test. The ICTY Chamber noted that the 'effective control' test is better applicable to private individuals engaged by a state to perform specific illegal acts in the territory of another state, while the 'overall control' test is better applicable to organized and hierarchically structured groups. The ICTY Appeals Chamber took the view that acts committed by Bosnian Serbs could come under the international responsibility of the Federal Republic of Yugoslavia (FRY as it then was) on the basis of the 'overall control' exercised by the FRY over the Republika Srpska and the VRS (army of the Republika Srpska), without there being any need to prove that each operation during which acts were committed in breach of international law was carried out on the FRY's instructions, or under its effective control.

Accordingly, in its *Tadic* judgment[202] the ICTY expressly adopted a conflicting view on the issue of use of control.[203] The Appeals Chamber of the ICTY argued that the ICJ's approach in *Nicaragua* was not 'persuasive' and was 'unconvincing' and went on to declare that the law was the contrary of what the ICJ had said it was.[204] In a subsequent case, the ICTY Appeals Chamber further declared that this contrary statement of the law had to be followed notwithstanding the asserted differences with the point of view of the ICJ.[205] Indeed, it could

---

198 See instrument establishing the ICTY, UN Security Council Resolution 827 (2003).

199 See website of ICTY at http://www.un.org/icty.

200 ICTY, *Tadic*.

201 ICJ, *Nicaragua v. US*, judgment of 27.6.1986.

202 ICTY Appeals Chamber, *Tadic*, judgment, 15.7.1999.

203 See for details: Shahabuddeen (2002).

204 ICTY Appeals Chamber, *Tadic, op cit.*, paras. 115, 116.

205 ICTY Appeals Chamber, *Aleksovski*, judgment of 24.3.2000, paras. 92 ff.

be argued that the test of control is variable, as in the *Celebici*[206] case, where the ICTY Appeals Chamber held that 'the 'overall control' test could be fulfilled even if the armed forces acting on behalf of the 'controlling state' had autonomous choices of means and tactics while participating in a common strategy along with the controlling State'.[207]

6.2 The ICJ's *Genocide Convention* judgment

In separate proceedings before the ICJ, Bosnia-Herzegovina, relying in particular on the Convention on the Prevention and Punishment of the Crime of Genocide 1948, argued that Serbia shared with the Republika Srpska the vision of a 'Greater Serbia' and consequently gave its support to those persons and groups responsible for the crimes which allegedly constituted genocide.[208] Bosnia-Herzegovina submitted that Serbia armed and equipped those persons and groups throughout the war and should therefore be held responsible. More specifically, Bosnia-Herzegovina urged the ICJ to apply the 'overall control' test used by the ICTY Appeals Chamber in the *Tadic* case instead of the 'effective control' test used in the ICJ's *Nicaragua* judgment.

The ICJ's starting point was the question of whether the massacre committed at Srebrenica in July 1995, which had been found to constitute the crime of genocide within the meaning of Articles II and III, paragraph (a) of the Convention on the Prevention and Punishment of the Crime of Genocide (1948)[209], were attributable in whole or in part to the Respondent, Serbia, alone at the time of the judgement.

This question actually has two aspects which must be discussed separately. First, it should be ascertained whether the acts committed at Srebrenica were perpetrated by organs of the Respondent, i.e. by persons or entities whose conduct is necessarily attributable to it, because they are in fact the instruments of its action. Next, if the preceding question is answered in the negative, it should be ascertained whether the acts in question were committed by persons

---

[206] ICTY, Appeals Chamber, *Prosecutor v. Zejnil Delalic, Zdravko Mucic (aka 'Pavo'), Hazim Delic and Esad Landzo (aka 'Zenga')*, judgment of 20.2.2001.

[207] *Ibid.*, para. 47.

[208] ICJ, *Bosnia-Herzegovina v. Serbia and Montenegro (Genocide Convention)*, judgment of 26.2.2007. See generally: Dimitrijevic / Milanovic (2008); Groome (2008); Rajkovic (2008).

[209] Article II of the Genocide Convention reads as follows:

'In the present Convention, genocide means any of the following acts committed with intent to destroy, in whole or in part, a national, ethnical, racial or religious group, as such: (a) killing members of the group'.

Article III of the Genocide Convention reads as follows:

'The following acts shall be punishable:

(a) genocide [...].'

who, while not organs of the Respondent, did nevertheless act on the instructions of, or under the direction or control of the Respondent.[210]

The first question was answered in the negative by the ICJ on the basis that the persons (Scorpions, Mladic) or entities (Republika Srpska and VRS) that committed the acts of genocide at Srebrenica did not have such ties with the FRY that they could be deemed to have been 'completely dependent'[211] on it. The ICJ also found that neither the Republika Srpska nor the VRS were *de jure* organs of the FRY since none of them had the status of organ of that state under its internal law. This conclusion was drawn by looking into Article 4 of the ILC Articles on state responsibility.[212]

Following the above conclusion, the ICJ had to determine whether the massacres at Srebrenica were committed by persons who, though not having the status of organs of the Respondent, nevertheless acted on its instructions or under its direction or control. In other words, the ICJ had to determine whether the perpetrators of the Srebrenica genocide could nevertheless be considered as *de facto* organs of the FRY. In order to do so, the ICJ looked at Article 8 of the ILC Articles on State Responsibility, which reads:

> 'The conduct of a person or group of persons shall be considered an act of a state under international law if the person or group of persons is *in fact acting on the instructions of, or under the direction or control of*, that state in carrying out the conduct.'[213] [emphasis added]

The ICJ then turned to its jurisprudence on the subject, in particular its *Nicaragua*[214] judgment. Confronted with the question of the responsibility of the US for actions by the Contras forces in Nicaragua, the ICJ held that there would be no state responsibility in the absence of evidence of actual 'effective control' of military operations, whereas the US would manifestly be answerable for the actions of its own armed forces and covert operations.[215] The test here was to prove that the persons who perpetrated the acts alleged to have violated international law did so in accordance with state instructions or under its 'effective control'. It

---

210 ICJ, *Genocide Convention, op cit.*

211 *Ibid.*, paras. 386 ff.

212 *Ibid.*

Article 4 of the ILC Articles on State Responsibility reads as follows:

'1. The conduct of any State organ shall be considered an act of that State under international law, whether the organ exercises legislative, executive, judicial or any other functions, whatever position it holds in the organization of the State, and whatever its character as an organ of the central Government or of a territorial unit of the State.

2. An organ includes any person or entity which has that status in accordance with the internal law of the State.'

213 Available at: http://untreaty.un.org/ilc/texts/instruments/english/draft%20articles/9_6_2001.pdf.

214 ICJ, *Nicaragua v. US, op cit.*

215 *Ibid.* para. 115.

must be shown that 'effective control' was used, or that the state's instructions were given in respect of each operation and not generally in respect of actions overall.

However, Bosnia-Herzegovina objected to this test in the circumstances of its case by raising the 'overall control' test used by the ICTY Appeals Chamber in the *Tadic* case mentioned above. But the ICJ strongly rejected the ICTY Appeal Chamber's 'reasoning' on the basis that findings on questions of state responsibility were outside the scope of the ICTY's jurisdiction, that jurisdiction being limited to individual responsibility. The ICJ went on to state that although it would accept the factual and legal findings made by the ICTY on the criminal liability of an accused, it would not accept its positions on issues of general international law, especially when they were outside its jurisdiction and unnecessary.[216]

The ICJ further argued that the 'overall control' test may be suitable to find whether or not an armed conflict is international, but that issue was not applicable to the current case and was therefore not considered.[217] Indeed, with respect to whether the 'overall control' test was applicable to find a state responsible for acts committed by armed forces which were not among its official organs, the ICJ emphasised that it found the argument 'unpersuasive'.[218] The ICJ continued its criticism of the ICTY by finding the overall control test 'unsuitable' and by qualifying it as a 'major drawback'.[219] In fact, according to the ICJ, the ICTY stretches 'too far, almost to breaking point, the connection which must exist between the conduct of a state's organs and its international responsibility'.[220]

By rejecting the ICTY's unauthorized 'overall control' test and applying its 'effective control' test, the ICJ was left with no option but to find that it had not been established that the massacres at Srebrenica were committed on the instructions, or under the direction of organs of the Respondent state, nor that the Respondent exercised effective control over the operations.

6.3 Commentary

The disagreement between the ICJ and ICTY on such a fundamental point of general international law, while operating under the same UN umbrella, must be considered to seriously undermine the consistency and uniformity of international law. In other words, the ICTY's *Tadic* and subsequent similar judgments, and the ICJ's *Genocide Convention* judgment further fragment the already divergent jurisprudence on this point. Moreover, it seems highly questionable whether the ICJ is indeed competent to limit the jurisdiction of the ICTY to factual and legal findings, it being an independent international

216 *Ibid.*, para. 403.

217 *Ibid.*, para. 404.

218 *Ibid.*

219 *Ibid.*, para 406.

220 *Ibid.*

tribunal. Indeed, the ICJ is effectively preventing the ICTY from expressing its own views on fundamental questions of general international law, which it considers necessary for rendering its judgments.

It is because of the lack of hierarchy between the ICJ and the ICTY, as compared for instance to the hierarchy between the ECJ and national courts of the EC Member States, that the ICJ is not in a position to establish such a hierarchy by imposing itself as the highest UN court regarding issues of general international law. Rather, any international court charged with applying a specific body of international law is authorised to apply rules belonging to other bodies of international law for the purpose of construing or applying a rule that is part of the corpus of legal rules on which it has primarily to decide upon. That authority is part and parcel of the inherent jurisdiction of any international court or tribunal.[221] Accordingly, as Cassese recently rightly pointed out, the ICJ was wrong to argue that the ICTY Appeals Chamber was outside the confines of its jurisdiction in dealing with an issue related to state responsibility.[222]

Obviously, in order to preserve the unity and consistency of international law, it is preferable that these courts and tribunals issue their judgments in accordance with the jurisprudence of the ICJ. But there may be good reasons to develop and apply different interpretations of international law in specific cases or areas of law which deviate from the ICJ's point of view. Indeed, it is submitted that the ICJ should respect the existing jurisdiction and expertise of specialised courts by showing more deference.

Moreover, as Cassese has rightly argued, the ICJ should not have confined its arguments to the effect that the *Tadic* case was about the nature of armed conflicts whereas the *Nicaragua* case revolved around state responsibility. According to Cassese, the two tests may coexist in that they relate to different subject matters.[223]

Finally, in this context one must refer to the dissenting opinion of ICJ judge and Vice-President Al-Khasawneh. He considered that the 'effective control' test for attribution established in the *Nicaragua* case is not suitable to questions of state responsibility for international crimes committed with a common purpose.[224] According to Al-Khasawneh, the 'overall control' test for attribution established in the *Tadic* case by the ICTY is more appropriate when the commission of international crimes is the common objective of the controlling state and the non-state actors.[225] The ICJ's refusal to infer genocidal intent from a consistent conduct in Bosnia and Herzegovina is inconsistent with the established jurisprudence of the ICTY.[226] In his explanation he went on to say that the ICJ had applied the 'effective control' test to a situation different from that presented

[221] Cassese (2007).

[222] *Ibid.*, 662.

[223] *Ibid.*, 663.

[224] See: ICJ Vice-President Al-Khasawneh, *Genocide Convention*, Dissenting Opinion.

[225] *Ibid.*

[226] *Ibid.*

in the *Nicaragua* case. In the present case, there was a unity of goals, unity of ethnicity and a common ideology, such that 'effective control' over non-state actors would not be necessary.[227] The ICJ's rejection of the standard in the *Tadic* case thus failed to address the crucial issue raised therein, namely that different types of activities, particularly given the ever-evolving nature of armed conflict, may call for subtle variations in the rules of attribution.[228] In his conclusion, he stated that the ICJ required too high a threshold for control, and one that did not accord with the facts of this case nor with the relevant jurisprudence of the ICTY.[229]

In sum, it is quite clear that with its 'ICTY bashing', the ICJ worsened rather than improved the situation regarding the already divergent approaches to the issue of state and individual responsibility. In fact, it would not be surprising if the ICTY or any other court (for instance the International Criminal Court (ICC)) that needed to deal with responsibility felt even less inclined to close this gap in future judgments when being criticized in this manner by the ICJ. Therefore, one can only hope, together with Cassese, that next time the ICJ will actually look into state practice and case law, instead of simply reiterating its own previous decisions.[230] That hope might however be vain if one agrees with Goldstone and Hamilton, who recently concluded that 'the ICJ was fairly measured in its response to the issue in Serbia-Bosnia.'[231]

7 The *Bosphorus* case

7.1 The factual and legal background

The *Bosphorus* case concerned the implementation of UN sanctions against former Yugoslavia. Bosphorus was leasing an airplane from the state-owned Yugoslav airline JAT. Because of UN sanctions[232], which were implemented by an EC Regulation[233], the plane was impounded by the Irish authorities. Bosphorus started proceedings against that measure which eventually reached the ECJ. Answering the preliminary questions posed by the Irish Supreme Court, the ECJ ruled that the measure was justified in order to reach the objectives of the UN sanctions – even though it imposed substantive limitations on Bosphorus' right to property.[234]

---

[227] *Ibid.*

[228] *Ibid.*

[229] *Ibid.*

[230] Cassese, *op cit.*, 668.

[231] Goldstone / Hamilton (2008) at 101. See also, in support of the ICJ's line of reasoning: Gattini (2007b).

[232] UN Security Council Resolution 820 (1993).

[233] EC Regulation 990/93, [1993] OJ L 102/14.

[234] Case C-84/95 *Bosphorus* [1996] ECR I-3953.

Following that ruling, Bosphorus started proceedings against Ireland before the ECrtHR, claiming that the measure violated its fundamental rights as protected by Article 1 of Protocol 1 to the ECHR, which protects the right to property. The ECrtHR was thus in effect called upon to review the EC measure and the ECJ's *Bosphorus* judgment. In other words, the question that arose was: which of the two courts is the supreme human rights court in Europe?[235]

7.2 The ECrtHR's *Bosphorus* judgment

After the ECrtHR had admitted the case in September 2001[236], it took almost 4 years for it to render its judgment.[237] It started its analysis by repeating the position it had already adopted in *Matthews*[238], that EC law measures could be reviewed – indirectly[239] – and that EC Member States could not hide behind an international organization. In other words, the EC Member States remain fully responsible for the effective protection of ECHR rights also vis-à-vis acts of IOs to which they have transferred competences.

However, in the *Bosphorus* case the ECrtHR shied away from actually reviewing whether or not Ireland had violated its ECHR obligations when implementing the UN and EC sanctions measures. Instead, it explicitly applied the *Solange* method for the first time *vis-à-vis* the ECJ.[240]

Accordingly, in a first step, the ECrtHR held that the level of fundamental rights protection, including the procedures available for obtaining judicial review before the ECJ within the EC is equivalent, though not identical, with the ECrtHR level.[241] Consequently, a presumption of sufficient fundamental rights

---

235 See generally: Canor, *supra* note 13; Douglas-Scott (2006a).

236 ECrtHR, *Bosphorus v. Ireland*, decision on admissibility of 13.9.2001.

237 ECrtHR, *Bosphorus v. Ireland*, judgment of 30.6.2005. See further: Douglas-Scott (2006b).

238 ECrtHR, *Matthews v. UK*, judgment of 18.2.1999.

239 See eg: ECrtHR, *Cantoni v. France*, judgment of 15.11.1996.

240 See regarding the *Solange* method: Jacqué (2005); Lavranos (2006b); *idem.*, (2008c).

241 ECrtHR, *Bosphorus v. Ireland, op. cit.*:

'155. In the Court's view, State action taken in compliance with such legal obligations is justified as long as the relevant organisation is considered to protect fundamental rights, as regards both the substantive guarantees offered and the mechanisms controlling their observance, in a manner which can be considered at least equivalent to that for which the Convention provides (see the above-cited M. & Co. decision, at p. 145, an approach with which the parties and the European Commission agreed). By 'equivalent' the Court means 'comparable': any requirement that the organisation's protection be 'identical' could run counter to the interest of international co-operation pursued (paragraph 150 above).
However, any such finding of equivalence could not be final and would be susceptible to review in the light of any relevant change in fundamental rights' protection.
156. If such equivalent protection is considered to be provided by the organisation, the presumption will be that a State has not departed from the requirements of the Convention when it does no more than implement legal obligations flowing from its membership of the organisation.
However, any such presumption can be rebutted if, in the circumstances of a particular case, it is

protection within the EC exists. In a second step, the ECrtHR explicitly held that as long as that level of fundamental rights protection is 'not manifestly deficient' in a specific case, the ECrtHR would not exercise its jurisdiction.[242] In other words, the ECrtHR will, in principle, refrain from reviewing EC law measures including ECJ judgments unless a specific case reveals a 'manifestly deficient' protection of fundamental rights within the EC.[243] Only in such a situation would the ECrtHR review EC law measures. Unfortunately, the ECrtHR did not define what 'manifestly deficient' actually means or when that threshold could be reached.[244]

In any case, the ECrtHR concluded that in this case there was no 'manifestly deficient' fundamental rights protection. Accordingly, the ECrtHR in substance rejected Bosphorus' claim.

7.3 Commentary

Quite obviously, the *Bosphorus* case was one of the most difficult judgments for the ECrtHR as it pushed the question of which court is the supreme fundamental rights court in Europe to the forefront. The underlying fundamental issue was of course nothing less than determining the jurisdictional relationship between the ECrtHR and the ECJ in a way that would preserve jurisdictional autonomy and, ultimately, the authority of both courts. In other words, the ECrtHR was called upon to carefully balance all the political, institutional and diplomatic interests that were involved.[245]

---

considered that the protection of Convention rights was manifestly deficient. In such cases, the interest of international co-operation would be outweighed by the Convention's role as a 'constitutional instrument of European public order' in the field of human rights (*Loizidou v Turkey* [preliminary objections], judgment of 23 March 1995, Series A No. 310, § 75).

[...]

165. In such circumstances, the Court finds that the protection of fundamental rights by EC law can be considered to be, and to have been at the relevant time, 'equivalent' (within the meaning of paragraph 155 above) to that of the Convention system. Consequently, the presumption arises that Ireland did not depart from the requirements of the Convention when it implemented legal obligations flowing from its membership of the EC (see paragraph 156).'

242 *Ibid*. See generally: Costello (2006); Heer-Reißmann (2006); Bröhmer (2006).

243 *Ibid*.: '166. The Court has had regard to the nature of the interference, to the general interest pursued by the impoundment and by the sanctions regime and to the ruling of the ECJ (in the light of the opinion of the Advocate General), a ruling with which the Supreme Court was obliged to and did comply. It considers it clear that there was no dysfunction of the mechanisms of control of the observance of Convention rights. In the Court's view, therefore, it cannot be said that the protection of the applicant's Convention rights was manifestly deficient with the consequence that the relevant presumption of Convention compliance by the respondent State has not been rebutted.'

244 Costello, *op cit*.

245 Kunoy / Dawes (2009); Harpaz (2009b).

The ECrtHR found a solution in the application of a sort of *Solange* method – comparable to the one used by the German Constitutional Court.[246] Since the *Solange* method will be discussed in more detail in the following Chapter, it suffices to note here that the ECrtHR found an elegant way to avoid reviewing ECJ judgments, while at the same time retaining its final jurisdiction over the ECJ for exceptional cases. In this way, the ECrtHR avoided a direct confrontation regarding its competing jurisdiction with the ECJ. Rather than claiming supreme final authority for adjudicating and determining fundamental rights in Europe, it gave the ECJ a *carte blanche* as far as fundamental rights issues that arise in the context of EC law are concerned. Obviously, the ECrtHR coupled this with the tacit understanding that the ECJ will take the ECrtHR jurisprudence fully into account.

On a more general level, in its *Bosphorus* ruling it seems that the ECrtHR has taken a step back from its bold *Matthews* ruling, in which it asserted a generally applicable indirect review of EC law measures, by making the 'manifestly deficient' test a condition before exercising its jurisdiction in cases involving EC law measures. Moreover, by combining the 'manifestly deficient' test with the *Solange* method, the ECrtHR demarcated its jurisdiction vis-à-vis the ECJ by *de facto* separating the fundamental rights protection in Europe into two distinctive zones – an EC law zone supervised by the ECJ and an ECHR law zone supervised by the ECrtHR. Accordingly, only in exceptional cases, that is, when the 'manifestly deficient' condition is met, would a case trespass from the EC law zone into the ECrtHR zone. In this way, the ECrtHR has been able to neatly compartmentalize the jurisdictions of both top European courts, thereby substantially reducing the risk of overlapping jurisdictions and potentially conflicting judgments.

In fact, with its recent *Kadi* judgment[247], where the ECJ entirely and forcefully rejected and overturned the CFI's *Kadi* judgment[248], which completely failed to provide for any kind of fundamental rights protection, the ECJ demonstrated to the ECrtHR that there is no need for concern about a potential 'manifestly deficient' fundamental rights standard within the Community legal order. Hence, there is no need for the ECrtHR to step in and exercise its jurisdiction should a case be brought before it. Indeed, it seems unlikely that the ECrtHR would exercise its jurisdiction now that the ECJ has demonstrated that it is actually willing to effectively apply the ECHR – also with regard to the implementation of UN sanctions.[249] Thus, the ECrtHR found in the *Solange* method a useful tool for managing its still unresolved and complex co-existence with the ECJ in an elegant and conflict-avoiding manner.

---

[246] See e.g.: Jacqué; Lavranos, *supra* note 240.

[247] Case C-402/05 P *Kadi v. Council* of 3.9.2008. See eg: Lavranos (2009a); Harpaz (2009a); Tridimas / Guitierrez-Fons (2009); Tridimas (2009); Heun-Rehn (2008); Graf Vitzhum (2008).

[248] Case T-315/01 *Kadi v Council* [2005] ECR II-3649. See e.g.: Eeckhout (2007); Lavranos (2006c).

[249] See further: Halberstam / Stein (2009).

However, the downside of the above is that, in principle, private parties (like Bosphorus) who were affected by UN sanctions, or rather the European or domestic implementation of them, are essentially prevented from obtaining judicial review from the ECrtHR in order to assess the conformity of the measures with the ECHR and the related jurisprudence of the ECrtHR if their case has been heard before by the CFI/ECJ.[250]

In sum, it appears that the ECrtHR managed to resolve the jurisdictional issue in a satisfactory way. However, the jurisdictional relationship between the ECrtHR and ECJ has still not been defined definitively, since the Lisbon Treaty – if and when it enters into force – explicitly provides for the accession of the EU to the ECHR, while at the same time making the Charter of Fundamental Rights legally binding within the Community legal order. As a result, two different legally-binding fundamental rights catalogues will exist and will be applied by the ECrtHR and the ECJ respectively. Obviously, the situation can only become more complicated in the future.[251]

8 Interim conclusions

The case studies presented in this Chapter illustrate that the issue of competing jurisdictions has been approached quite differently by different courts and tribunals, resulting in the effect of either more fragmentation or more unification. At one end of the spectrum, we find the OSPAR Arbitral Tribunal, the ECJ's judgment in the *MOX plant* dispute, the WTO panel and Appellate Body rulings in *Mexico soft drinks* and *Brazilian Tyres* and the ICJ's *Genocide* judgment, which all showed little concern for the possible jurisdiction of the other court or tribunal involved in the dispute. At the other end of the spectrum, are the UNCLOS Arbitral Tribunal and the WTO panel in *Brazilian Tyres,* which respected the jurisdiction of the other court/tribunal by either staying the proceedings and allowing the other court/tribunal to express its view regarding jurisdictional competition, or by accepting the decision rendered by the other court/tribunal as a fact of the case and taking it fully into account. The ECrtHR's *Bosphorus* judgment also belongs to this category in that it shows respect for the ECJ's jurisdiction, while at the same time keeping a reserve jurisdiction in order to be able to interfere in the ECJ's jurisdiction if necessary. In the middle of the spectrum, we find the *IJzeren Rijn* Arbitral Tribunal, which, while discussing the possibility that the ECJ might have jurisdiction in the dispute, eventually concluded on the basis of a flawed analysis that the ECJ has no jurisdiction and therefore rendered its award. The *IJzeren Rijn* Arbitral Tribunal did however at least pay lip service to the issue of jurisdictional competition.

The different approaches of the various courts and tribunals can to a certain extent be explained by the sometimes significant differences regarding their

[250] See generally: Lindner (2007).

[251] See further: Lavranos (2008b).

legal foundation, tasks, functions and scope of jurisdiction. For example, the ECJ is a permanent court that is predominantly interested in protecting its exclusive jurisdiction and ensuring the consistency of the Community legal order. In addition, through the preliminary ruling system, it is able to ensure in a legally binding way that all national courts of the EC Member States follow ECJ jurisprudence. In contrast, ad hoc arbitral tribunals that are established to resolve a specific dispute are only interested in deciding the case according to the specific parameters defined by the parties, without having to take other systemic issues into account.

Moreover, the legal orders or legal regimes that are involved in overlapping jurisdictions differ in the various cases. For instance, in the *MOX plant* case, UNCLOS provisions overlapped with EC law provisions, whereas in the *Mexican soft drinks* and *Brazilian Tyres* cases regional trade law provisions were in competition with global WTO law provisions. One could classify theses examples as *vertical hierarchical relationships* in which the application of similar norms emanating from different legal sources was at issue, whereas in the *Genocide Convention* and *Tadic* cases, the same general rules or principles of public international law were applied by both courts. This situation could thus be classified as a *horizontal relationship* involving the divergent application of the same norm by courts and tribunals that act under the same UN law umbrella.

However, despite these differences in terms of their foundation, tasks, function and scope of jurisdiction, there is one fundamental problem that is common to all the cases, namely the lack of any formal legally binding institutional coordination between international courts and tribunals.[252] To be sure, competing jurisdiction as such could be seen as unproblematic, indeed one may even sympathize with the view recently posited by Professor Cogan, who argues that even more jurisdictional competition is needed in order to constrain the expanding power of international courts and tribunals.[253] Nevertheless, the case studies discussed in this Chapter quite clearly exemplify the fundamental problems that have so far arisen from jurisdictional competition.[254]

In the first place, we have noted the creation of legal inconsistencies resulting from either conflicting interpretation of the law or failure to fully take it, or the jurisprudence of other courts and tribunals (potentially) involved in a dispute, into account. This in turn has had a fragmenting effect on the legal systems and/or subsystems involved.

In the second place, several cases appear as clear examples of forum shopping, which results in endless re-litigation, further delaying a final and definitive solution of disputes. This, moreover, not only contributes to a huge and unnecessary investment in resources (money, manpower and time), but also to damage to the political and economic relationships between the parties involved.

[252] See generally: Sauer, *supra* note 26.

[253] Cogan (2008).

[254] On the more general negative effects of fragmentation see: Benvenisti / Downs (2007).

This is an important, but often underestimated cause, or root of, even more disputes between parties that have been entangled in protracted proceedings.

In the third place, jurisdictional competition that has led to divergent or conflicting rulings or to open ignorance of the existing jurisdiction of another court/tribunal undermines the authority of the courts and tribunals themselves, in particular if they openly criticize each other as has happened between the ICJ and ICTY. One should not underestimate the negative impression that is created by such behaviour not only on government officials but also upon lawyers and academics and the public at large.

In the fourth place, it should also be remembered that divergent or conflicting rulings by different courts or tribunals create conflicting obligations for the parties involved, which inevitably forces states to breach one or the other law. This in turn undermines respect for and belief in justice, the rule of law and peaceful dispute resolution.

However, to conclude on a more positive note, the ECrtHR's application of the *Solange* method points towards a possible solution which can reduce or even eliminate the problems associated with competing jurisdictions. Indeed, as will be explained in more detail in the next Chapter, a consistent and uniform application of the *Solange* method by all international courts and tribunals would substantially reduce the risk of fragmentation of the international legal order (including regional legal orders). It would also foster and improve understanding and informal cooperation between international courts and judges.[255]

---

[255] On this aspect generally, see: Slaughter, *supra* note 41.

CHAPTER 4

Possible Solutions

Following the analysis of several case studies which have illustrated various consequences of competing jurisdictions, this Chapter will look at some of the possible solutions for avoiding competing jurisdictions, or at least mitigating the negative effects associated with the problem.[256] For better understanding, the Chapter makes a rough distinction between hard-law and soft-law options.

1 Hard law options

Hard-law options refer to possible solutions by way of formal legally-binding techniques that would regulate the jurisdictional relationship between international courts and tribunals and/or the choices of parties in selecting a certain dispute settlement body.

As has been pointed out before, one of the main weaknesses of the current situation at the international level is the lack of any formal hierarchical or otherwise formally coordinated relationship between the increasing number of international courts and tribunals. Accordingly, the first, obvious, solution would be to make the ICJ the true supreme international court with the authority to give final and authoritative interpretations on fundamental points of public international law that would also bind the other international courts and tribunals. In the past, several proposals have been put forward to this effect.

1.1 Extending the jurisdiction of the ICJ

Even though the UN Charter describes the ICJ as the principle judicial organ, the truth is that currently only 66 out of some 192 UN member states have accepted the jurisdiction of the ICJ, many with substantial reservations.[257] Moreover, the jurisdiction of the ICJ is very limited, in particular compared to the ECJ, both in terms of *ratio personae* and *ratio materae,* as well as in terms of the present optional acceptance of its jurisdiction by states. Therefore, an extension of its current jurisdiction would seem to be an obvious solution.[258] If the ICJ were converted into the supreme international court, it could be put into a position to ensure uniformity and consistency within the jurisprudence of the various international courts and tribunals much more than now. This would, however, on the one hand require that all states accept its full and compulsory jurisdiction, and on the other hand that all other international courts and tribunals be bound – in principle – to follow, or at least to take into account, its jurisprudence. However, as the *Tadic* and *Genocide Convention* cases illustrate, it is already very difficult for both the ICTY and the ICJ to apply the same legal rule congruently.

---

[256] For a recent analysis of the various possible solutions see: Linton / Kebede Tiba (2009).

[257] See: http://www.icj-cij.org/jurisdiction/index.php?p1=5&p2=1&p3=3.

[258] See generally: Sugihara (2002).

1.2 Making the ICJ a Court of Appeal vis-à-vis the other courts and tribunals

Along these lines, one could think of making the ICJ a Court of Appeal vis-à-vis the other international courts and tribunals. In this way, the ICJ would be the ultimate arbiter regarding aspects of public international law. Accordingly, it would be in a position to provide binding interpretations and thus ensure homogeneity in the application of public international law. In other words, a clear hierarchical structure would be introduced in which the ICJ would be above the other international courts and tribunals. The ICJ could fill the role of Court of Appeal particularly effectively if it became a compulsory Court of Appeal for all international courts and tribunals. This, however, would require the extension of the scope of its jurisdiction in terms of *ratio personae* and *ratio materae* so that also natural and legal persons would have *locus standi,* as is the case with several international courts and tribunals. A less far-reaching option would be to establish a Court of Appeal hierarchy on a case by case basis and for a limited number of international courts/tribunals, for instance the ITLOS, the ICC and the ICTY.

1.3 Creating a preliminary ruling system for the ICJ

Another way of establishing a hierarchical structure between the ICJ and the other international courts and tribunals would be the creation of a preliminary ruling system like the one established in the Community legal order (Art. 234 EC).[259] This would mean that the ICJ would be able to receive requests for preliminary rulings on issues of public international law from other international courts and tribunals which consider its guidance necessary in order to render their decisions. In this way, the ICJ would be able to ensure a high level of uniformity of international law while at the same time leaving the other international courts and tribunals sufficient freedom to decide specific cases in accordance with the respective requirements.

One could indeed go a step further by creating a system by which the ICJ would also be able to request preliminary rulings from the other international courts and tribunals, for instance from the ICC on aspects of criminal law, or from the ITLOS on the law of the sea. In this way, the uniformity of international law could be ensured even better. Compared with the formal Court of Appeal system suggested above, the preliminary ruling system would impose a less strict hierarchical relationship as every international court/tribunal would decide for itself on a case-by-case basis whether or not a preliminary ruling were indeed necessary. Moreover, the creation of a preliminary ruling system would also enhance communication and co-operation between the ICJ and the other international courts and tribunals, which in turn could further strengthen the

[259] See: Pellet (2004); Guillaume (1995).

uniformity and consistency of international law by reducing the risk of conflicting judgments on the same issues.

In this context, one could even take a further step by also including regional courts in this preliminary ruling system, so that the ECJ, the ECrtHR, the Inter-American Human Rights Court, and the African Human Rights Court would also be able to request preliminary rulings from the ICJ.

1.4 Extending the already existing advisory jurisdiction of the ICJ

A less far-reaching proposal is that to extend the already existing advisory jurisdiction of the ICJ by broadening the group of organs and bodies that could request an advisory opinion from it.[260] According to Article 65 of the Statute of the ICJ, the ICJ may give an advisory opinion on any legal question at the request of any body that may be authorized by, or in accordance with, the UN Charter to make such a request. Currently, 21 duly authorized UN organs and agencies are allowed to request an Advisory opinion. These include all the principal organs of the UN (with the exception of the Secretary General representing the UN Secretariat), the 16 UN Specialized Agencies and the Interim Committee of the General Assembly. These are the only organizations having 'standing' in advisory proceedings before the ICJ. The UN Security Council and General Assembly have the authority to request advisory opinions on any legal question, while the other organizations may request advisory opinions only on legal questions arising within the scope of their activities. Extending the number of bodies allowed to request an advisory opinion would be particularly useful because advisory opinions of the ICJ have been very influential in determining a number of fundamental aspects of international law.[261] Moreover, this proposal is particularly attractive as it would involve comparatively few changes to the UN Charter and ICJ Statute. At the same time, however, the hierarchical structure would remain quite loose, so that the ability of the ICJ to ensure a high level of uniformity in the interpretation of international law would continue to be limited.

1.5 Creating a *Tribunal des Conflits*

Another idea is the creation of a *Tribunal des Conflits*. This idea has been borrowed from the French judicial system, which many decades ago created a *Tribunal des Conflits* in order to resolve jurisdiction disputes between the two main branches of law over certain cases.[262] The French *Tribunal des Conflits* is composed of three members of the *Conseil d'Etat* (supreme administrative

[260] Dupuy (1999).

[261] See: Aljaghoub (2006); Hirsch (2005).

[262] It should be noted that such a court is known in other jurisdictions as well. For instance, in Israel there is a similar court that determines jurisdictional conflicts between religious courts.

court), three members of the *Cour de Cassation* (supreme civil/criminal court) and two other members. In other words, the *Tribunal des Conflits* is composed of judges from the two supreme courts and has the task to decide which of the courts has jurisdiction to adjudicate a case when both branches of courts (the administrative and the civil/criminal branch) claim jurisdiction over the same case. At the international law level, one could imagine a *Tribunal des Conflits de jurisdiction international* – composed of several members of the ICJ (for instance six ICJ judges) and 5 members of the other international courts and tribunals (one ICTY judge, one ICC judge, one ITLOS judge, one PCA member and one WTO Appellate Body member) plus one independent member (an internationally recognized international law professor), who would come together in order to determine *in fine* which court/tribunal has jurisdiction in a certain case and to give final interpretations on issues of international law that have been interpreted differently by the various international courts/tribunals. The advantage of this proposal would be that the creation of a new overarching tribunal would allow for a tailor-made and flexible statute that would serve the needs, instead of trying to reform with great difficulty, the currently existing system. Moreover, the equal participation of the other international courts and tribunals in such a *Tribunal des Conflits* would ensure a constant exchange of ideas and lead to compromises that would find the support of all international courts and tribunals. Accordingly, a high level of acceptance of a uniform interpretation of international law aspects could be secured with relatively little legal complication.

1.6 Explicitly defining the scope of jurisdiction in founding instruments

Finally, another way of dealing with competing jurisdictions is to expressly regulate the scope of the jurisdiction of international courts and tribunals in their founding instruments. A number of options are of course possible.[263]

First, an exclusive jurisdiction provision, similar to Article 292 EC, could be inserted into each founding instrument requiring state parties involved in a dispute to bring a particular dispute exclusively before the designated court or tribunal.

Second, the relevant rules of procedures of courts and tribunals could explicitly prescribe the mandatory application of principles such as *res judicata* and *lis pendens*.[264] The principle of *res judicata* essentially aims to prevent parties to a dispute from re-litigating the same dispute or the same legal issue before another court or tribunal. The principle of *lis pendes* means that while a case or dispute is pending before one court or tribunal, another court or tribunal that is faced with the same dispute should stay the proceedings until the first issues its judgment. In that way, the second court can either refuse to exercise its jurisdiction or take the first court's decision into account. Both principles

[263] See generally: Cannizzaro (2007).

[264] Both principles will be discussed in more detail in the soft-law section below.

are often used, in particular, in private international law, ICSID and investor-state cases. Therefore, most international courts and tribunals are familiar with these principles, so that the mandatory prescription of their application should not pose a problem for them. Indeed, a formal prescription of these principles in the rules of procedure would probably help to reduce the risk of divergent or conflicting judgments by different courts or tribunals which are faced with the same dispute or legal issue.

Unfortunately however, all the hard-law options discussed above face several obstacles that make them *de facto* impossible to implement in practice.

In the first place, they would require a huge effort both in reorganizing and expanding the ICJ's capacities, as well as to create a wider general acceptance of its jurisdiction. Quite clearly, there is currently no such support among the international community. Indeed, the US has recently shown particularly strong disrespect for the authority of the ICJ, which obviously hinders any major improvements in its capacities.[265]

In the second place, the options would require the modification of existing treaty instruments or the drawing up of new instruments, both of which would require ratification by all state parties. This would obviously be a very time-consuming and complex process.

In the third place, it may be doubted whether the other international courts and tribunals would accept a *primus inter pares* position of the ICJ. Moreover, it is questionable whether the ICJ would be able to address all the different issues of international law with sufficient expertise, particularly regarding the more specialized areas such as environmental or criminal law.

In sum, it must be concluded that even though the hard-law options promise to be able to regulate competing jurisdictions effectively, because of the practical difficulties involved in their actual implementation, one must look further, to soft-law options.

2 Soft-law options

The soft-law options refer to methods occasionally applied by courts and tribunals to deal with competing jurisdictions – without them being formally required to do so.

2.1 The *res judicata* and *lis pendens* principles

As mentioned above, the *res judicata* and *lis pendens* principles are widely – though not systematically – used by many courts and tribunals in dealing with jurisdictional issues.

[265] Reference is made to the withdrawal of the US's acceptance of ICJ jurisdiction regarding the Vienna Convention on Diplomatic Protection 1961 after the ICJ had issued several judgments against the US concerning the execution of death penalties. See generally: Paulus (2004).

The *res judicata* principle allows a court to decline jurisdiction on the basis of an earlier ruling by another court or tribunal on the same matter. In other words, it ensures the finality of proceedings by excluding a re-litigation of the same dispute before another court/tribunal.[266] The *lis pendens* principle bars proceedings before a court as long as the same claim is pending before another court/tribunal.[267] In this context, it should be emphasized that there can be no doubt that the *res judicata* and *lis pendens* principles are also applicable in international judicial proceedings.[268] However, there are three conditions for their application in both cases: (i) identity of parties, (ii) identity of object or subject matter, i.e. exactly the same issue must be in question, (iii) identity of the legal cause of action. It is obvious that the second and third conditions in particular raise difficulties in ascertaining whether or not they are fulfilled in a given case.[269] Moreover, even if a court/tribunal concludes that a relevant earlier decision of another court/tribunal indeed exists, it could still decide to proceed with the case as it is not *legally* bound to take the other decision into account. Nonetheless, the application of the *res judicata* and *lis pendens* principles could certainly help reduce the number of conflicting judgments by denying parties the possibility of re-litigating the same dispute in the hope of a different outcome. Furthermore, respect for and acceptance of a final decision by an international court/tribunal increases legal certainty, and also enhances the authority and credibility of the various international courts and tribunals in general.[270]

2.2 The principle of good faith

The principle of good faith, which in international law is usually applied to state obligations, is considered here more broadly and thus also applied to international courts and tribunals when they apply and develop international law. It has been argued that all judicial bodies have a *legal* duty to take the decisions of other international courts/tribunals on the same issue into account and to act in good faith, i.e. to follow those decisions unless there are overwhelming reasons, which should in turn be clearly set out by the court that wishes to deviate, for not doing so.[271] According to this approach, this legal obligation flows from the need to ensure consistency within the system of international law in which all international courts and tribunals operate.[272]

Although, this approach fits nicely with the idea of a global community of courts as posited by Anne-Marie Slaughter[273], the problem is that the obligation is a *moral* rather than a legal one and that – due to the lack of any hierarchical

[266] See generally: Söderlund (2005); Reinisch (2004).

[267] See further: Shany, *op cit.*, 212 ff.

[268] Reinisch, *op cit.*, 47-50.

[269] *Ibid.*, 55 ff.

[270] See further: Shany, *op cit.*, 170 ff.

[271] See: Martinez, *op cit.*, 487 ff.; Shahabuddeen, *op.cit.*

[272] Shahabuddeen, *op cit.*, 646-647.

[273] See: Slaughter, *op cit.*, Chapter 2.

order between the various international courts/tribunals – nothing can prevent an international court/tribunal from deviating, for instance, from the case law of the ICJ.

Nonetheless, it is submitted that all international courts and tribunals have a special responsibility to ensure systemic coherence within the international legal order and its specialized sub-legal regimes as much as possible.

2.3 Comity

Another soft-law option that has been widely discussed is comity, which is considered to be one of the most promising tools for reducing the negative effects associated with jurisdictional competition. To use the words of Professor Yuval Shany, comity can

> 'create a framework for jurisdictional interaction that will enable courts and tribunals to apply rules originating in other judicial institutions. This, in turn, will encourage cross-fertilization and may result in increased legitimacy of international judgments (through utilizing the authority of other international courts and tribunals) and in the application of the "best available" rule, reflecting not merely the narrow interests of the parties and the law-applying regime at hand but also those of the international community at large.'[274]

Professor Shany defines comity as follows:

> 'According to this principle, which is found in many countries (mostly from common law systems) courts in one jurisdiction should respect and demonstrate a degree of deference to the law of other jurisdictions, including the decisions of judicial bodies operating in the jurisdictions.'[275]

In this context, it should be noted that the terms 'comity', 'international comity' or 'judicial comity' are often used interchangeably and are, moreover, amorphous and applied in very different contextual settings.[276] Therefore, it is interesting to examine the origin and nature of comity a bit closer. According to Professor Shany, comity originates in common law jurisdictions. Indeed, already in 1895 in *Hilton v. Guyo* the US Supreme Court argued with respect to foreign acts that

> '"comity", in the legal sense, is neither a matter of absolute obligation, on the one hand, nor of mere courtesy and good will, upon the other. But it is the recognition which one nation allows within its territory to the legislative, executive or judicial acts of another nation.'[277]

[274] *Ibid.*, 261.

[275] *Ibid.*, 260.

[276] See e.g.: Ramsey (1998); Perez (1998); Ben-Ezer / Bendor (2003); Foster Halabi (2005); Tan (2005).

[277] US Supreme Court, *Hilton v. Guyot*, 159 U.S. 113, 163-64 (1895).

More recently, the US Supreme Court has emphasized the need to extend judicial cooperation to quasi-judicial international tribunals as well.[278] Accordingly, viewed from this perspective comity is not considered as a legal principle *stricto senso*, but rather a kind of 'gentlemen's agreement' between courts and tribunals. In other words, every court or tribunal is totally free to decide whether or not to apply comity in a certain case and what consequence to attach to it.

However, if basic international law instruments are taken into account, which is appropriate since we are dealing here with comity between international courts and tribunals, one can find strong evidence for the argument that comity has passed the level of being merely a soft-law tool. For example, Article 1 (1) of the UN Charter explicitly notes that the purposes of the UN are:

> '1. To maintain international peace and security, and to that end: to take effective collective measures for the prevention and removal of threats to the peace, and for the suppression of acts of aggression or other breaches of the peace, and to bring about by *peaceful means, and in conformity with the principles of justice and international law, adjustment or settlement of international disputes* or situations which might lead to a breach of the peace;' [emphasis added]

This directly applies to all courts and tribunals established by the United Nations (e.g. the ICJ, ICTY), and arguably also to all other international courts and tribunals that are called upon to apply the UN Charter.

Similarly, the Preamble of the Vienna Convention on the Law of Treaties (VCLT) of 1969 explicitly states:

> 'Affirming that disputes concerning treaties, like other international disputes, should be settled by peaceful means and *in conformity with the principles of justice and international law*'. [emphasis added]

Since the VCLT is generally considered to be (partly) an expression of customary international law[279], the principles of justice and international law apply to all international disputes. This has also been confirmed by the UN General Assembly, which adopted an Outcome document at the 2005 World Summit.[280] The document explicitly states:

> 'Pacific settlement of disputes
>
> 73. We emphasize the obligation of States to settle their disputes by peaceful means in accordance with Chapter VI of the Charter, including, when appropriate, by the *use of the International Court of Justice*. All States should act in accordance with the Declaration on Principles of International Law concerning Friendly Relations and Cooperation among States in accordance with the Charter of the United Nations. [emphasis added]

[278] US Supreme Court, *Intel Corp. v. Advanced Micro Devices*, 542 U.S. 241 (2004).

[279] See e.g.: Shaw (2008) 903.

[280] 2005 World Summit Outcome, G.A. Res. 60/1, paras. 73, 134, U.N. Doc. A/RES/60/1 (25.10. 2005).

> [. . .]
> Rule of law
> 134. *Recognizing the need for universal adherence to and implementation of the rule of law at both the national and international levels* [emphasis added],
> we:
> (*a*) Reaffirm our commitment to the purposes and principles of the Charter and international law and to an *international order based on the rule of law* and international law, which is essential for peaceful coexistence and cooperation among States; [emphasis added]
> [. . .]
> (*f*) Recognize the *important role of the International Court of Justice, the principal judicial organ of the United Nations, in adjudicating disputes among States and the value of its work, call upon States that have not yet done so to consider accepting the jurisdiction of the Court in accordance with its Statute and consider means of strengthening the Court's work*, including by supporting the Secretary-General's Trust Fund to Assist States in the Settlement of Disputes through the International Court of Justice on a voluntary basis.' [emphasis added]

Hence, when international courts and tribunals are called upon to resolve an international dispute, they must do so in conformity with the principles of justice and international law. Indeed, it is submitted that comity is part of the principles of justice. More specifically, it is argued that comity must be understood as being an inherent part of the tasks and functions of a judge or arbitrator to resolve disputes in conformity with the principles of justice and international law.[281]

Thus, comity can be seen to be an integral part of the obligation of all international courts and tribunals, and therefore must always be applied when such courts and tribunals are determining whether or not to exercise their jurisdiction in a specific case brought before them. In other words, as Professor Petersmann has recently and convincingly argued, judicial comity must be considered to be part of the rule of law and of delivering justice by judges and arbitrators when resolving a dispute.[282] Furthermore, it is submitted that all international courts and tribunals have an obligation to ensure the efficiency and coherence of the international legal order when executing their functions.[283]

If this point of view is accepted, the question arises as to what this duty entails for the judges and arbitrators. Essentially, it means delivering justice towards: (i) the parties involved in a dispute, (ii) other international courts and tribunals, and (iii) the rule of law.

Justice towards the parties means that every court or tribunal is obliged to resolve a dispute by rendering a decision that is efficient, fair and final. Thus, parties must be discouraged from endlessly re-litigating the same dispute (or parts of the same dispute), while at the same time be encouraged to end their

281 Petersmann (2007b).

282 *Ibid.*

283 Leathley (2007).

disputes by accepting the outcome of the first proceeding. Since the court or tribunal first seized of a dispute can substantially determine the process, it bears particular responsibility when deciding whether or not to exercise its jurisdiction.

However, at the same time, courts and tribunals must exercise their jurisdiction in a way that does not undermine the authority of the other courts and tribunals whose jurisdiction is also potentially triggered. So justice towards other international courts or tribunals entails showing respect for another court's jurisdiction by relinquishing a court's own jurisdiction, staying the proceedings, or taking full account of the other court's decision.

This brings us to the third element of justice, and that is to show justice towards international law, more specifically by preserving its uniform and effective application.

In short, the systematic application of comity and its inherent obligations for all courts and tribunals appears to indeed be a very useful tool in regulating overlapping jurisdictions in an amicable and systemic way. However, as we have seen, the case studies show that not all courts and tribunals have yet fully embraced comity as an obligatory fundamental tool to be applied systematically.

2.4 The *Solange* method

Building on the comity principle, the *Solange* method has recently been explicitly applied by the ECrtHR to delineate its jurisdiction from the ECJ's jurisdiction. This is a first example of the method being elevated from its vertical origins, i.e. regulating the jurisdictional relationship between the German Constitutional Court and the ECJ, and applied to the horizontal relationship between the two supreme European courts. Accordingly, it seems an interesting exercise to apply the *Solange* method in those case studies in which it was not applied, and to find out what the effects of its application would have been, in particular regarding the regulation of jurisdictional issues. However, before doing so, it seems appropriate to outline the origins of the *Solange* method.

2.4.1 The origins of the *Solange* method

The *Solange* method was invented by the German Federal Constitutional Court (Bundesverfassungsgericht (BVerfG)) in order to regulate its jurisdiction vis-à-vis the ECJ. For our purposes it suffices to focus on a few key aspects of the BVerfG's *Solange* jurisprudence.[284]

In the first place, it should be noted that the development of this jurisprudence, which dates back to the first *Solange* judgment in 1974,[285] has not been linear, but rather has been wavelike, with high and low points. The high points are the times in which the BVerfG was prepared to give up more of its 'reserve

[284] See more extensively: Lavranos, *supra* note 240.

[285] BVerfGE 37, 327 *Solange I*.

jurisdiction'; the low points those when the BVerfG assumed or reassumed more jurisdictional powers.

In the second place, it should be remembered that the *Solange* method was introduced because the supremacy claim of the ECJ coupled with the expanding development of Community law collided with the protection of fundamental rights as guaranteed by the national constitutions of member states. In particular, the BVerfG considered fundamental rights a 'no-go area' for the ECJ. In this area, the BVerfG always maintained a 'reserve jurisdiction', in the sense that it considered itself at all times competent to exert its jurisdiction, despite the existence and use of ECJ jurisdiction (which in the eyes of the ECJ is exclusive).

The *Solange I* case concerned the question of what domestic courts should do in the case of a conflict between a provision of an EC Regulation and fundamental rights as protected by the German Constitution. The BVerfG held that *as long as* (which in German is 'solange') the integration process of the EC does not contain a catalogue of fundamental rights which is adequate to the German Constitution and has been duly approved by the German Parliament, a German court may, after requesting a preliminary ruling from the ECJ, request a ruling from the BVerfG as to the compatibility of the EC measure with the German Constitution.[286] In substance, the BVerfG concluded that in this case there was no conflict between the EC measure and the German Constitution. Nonetheless, the BVerfG found it necessary to emphasise that it did not consider the level of fundamental rights protection at EC level to be adequate enough, in particular because no EC catalogue of fundamental rights, which could be compared to the one in the German Constitution, existed at EC level. Consequently, since at that time fundamental rights had not been explicitly recognized in the jurisprudence of the ECJ, the BVerfG considered itself unable to give up its jurisdiction regarding fundamental rights protection in favour of exclusive ECJ jurisdiction.

That signal from the BVerfG was subsequently picked up by the ECJ, which started to develop a jurisprudence on fundamental rights protection.[287] In recognition of that development, the BVerfG conceded parts of its jurisdiction under certain conditions when it issued its second *Solange* judgment in 1986.[288] In this case the main issue was whether a judgment of the ECJ on the interpretation and application of EC law must be considered to be final or whether it could still be reviewed by the BVerfG if a conflict with fundamental rights as protected by the German Constitution could be established. In its *Solange II* judgment, the BVerfG held that as long as the case law of the ECJ offered effective protection of fundamental rights against the acts of public organs (i.e. EC organs), which is comparable to the minimum level as guaranteed by the German Constitution, the BVerfG will not exercise its jurisdiction in reviewing EC law measures.[289] In other words, the BVerfG accepted that the interpretation of the ECJ regarding

[286] *Ibid.* para. 56.

[287] See eg: Case 4/73 *Nold* [1974] ECR 491; Case 44/79 *Hauer* [1979] ECR 3727.

[288] BVerfGE 73, 339 *Solange II.*

[289] *Ibid.*, para. 132.

EC law is authoritative and final, and thus also binding on all German courts – including the BVerfG itself.

So, after *Solange II*, the relationship between the ECJ and the BVerfG was back on track. Indeed, the ECJ continued its approach of explicitly integrating fundamental rights into the Community legal order by issuing several bold judgments on the subject[290] (despite or because of the lack of a written catalogue of EC fundamental rights). However, it must be highlighted at the same time that the ECJ did not go as far as to submit itself to the jurisdiction of the ECrtHR when it rejected the possibility of EC accession to the ECHR in its Opinion 2/94.[291]

However, in 1992 the Maastricht Treaty came onto the European stage and introduced new tensions into the ECJ/BVerfG relationship. Although the Maastricht Treaty certified ECJ jurisprudence on fundamental rights protection, by explicitly referring to the fundamental rights as protected by the common constitutional traditions of the member states and the ECHR in the EU Treaty,[292] the other novel and far-reaching components of the Treaty—the EMU and the Euro, Common Foreign and Security Policy and Police and Justice Cooperation—were for the BVerfG too much to swallow. Hence, in its *Solange III* judgment the BVerfG *de facto* overturned its *Solange II* jurisprudence by allowing for the non-application of EC law in Germany under certain conditions (the so called *ausbrechender Gemeinschaftsakt*).[293]

---

290 See eg: Case C-260/89 *ERT* [1991] ECR I-2925; Case 5/88 *Wachauf* [1989] ECR 2609. See generally: Weiler (1996).

291 Opinion 2/94 *Accession to the ECHR* [1996] ECR I-1759.

292 See Articles 6 and 46 of the Treaty of the European Union (TEU) adopted 7.2.1992, entered into force 1.11.1993). Article 6 TEU reads as follows:

1. The Union is founded on the principles of liberty, democracy, respect for human rights and fundamental freedoms, and the rule of law, principles which are common to the Member States.

2. The Union shall respect fundamental rights, as guaranteed by the European Convention for the Protection of Human Rights and Fundamental Freedoms signed in Rome on 4 November 1950 and as they result from the constitutional traditions common to the Member States, as general principles of Community law.'

[...]

Article 46 TEU reads as follows:

The provisions of the Treaty establishing the European Community, the Treaty establishing the European Coal and Steel Community and the Treaty establishing the European Atomic Energy Community concerning the powers of the Court of Justice of the European Communities and the exercise of those powers shall apply only to the following provisions of this Treaty:

[...]

(d) Article 6(2) [TEU] with regard to action of the institutions, in so far as the Court has jurisdiction under the Treaties establishing the European Communities under this Treaty;

[...].

293 In its BVerfGE 89, 155 *Solange III* decision, the BVerfG defined the conditions of 'ausbrechender Gemeinschaftsakt' as follows (at para. 106): If European organs applied and developed the EU Treaty in

Thus, in its third *Solange* judgment, on the Maastricht Treaty, the BVerfG, while allowing the ratification of the Maastricht Treaty by Germany, made clear that the future development of the EU remains under the conditional approval of the BVerfG. Thus, it reasserted its 'reserve jurisdiction' and signalled to the ECJ that it was prepared to question the doctrine of supremacy of EC law and consequently the authority of the ECJ. In other words, the BVerfG challenged the ECJ's self-declared supremacy over national laws and institutions, the impact of which largely depends on voluntary submission by national courts. At that time, the relationship between the BVerfG and the ECJ had become somewhat frosty—to say the least.

The vigilant attitude taken by the BVerfG towards the ECJ was justified, at least from its own perspective (as well as that of much of German academia) by the position adopted by the ECJ and the Court of First Instance (CFI) towards the EC 'banana regulation' and its inconsistency with WTO law.[294] In short, German importers claimed that the EC banana regulation essentially disrupted their import opportunities because it made their imports from Central and South America much more expensive. This, the importers argued, constituted a violation of their fundamental rights over property. Moreover, they argued that the inconsistency of the banana regulation with WTO law, which is an inconsistency of a lower norm (EC banana regulation) with a higher norm (EC Treaty, ECHR), could not be accepted on the basis of the rule of law and the ECHR. However, the ECJ and CFI were not prepared to review the compatibility of the EC banana regulation with WTO law or the fundamental rights protected by the ECHR and/or national constitutions.[295] Thus, they left the EC banana regulation intact.

Moreover, in parallel proceedings before German courts, the importers claimed that this also constituted a violation of the German ratification act of the EC Treaty and should therefore be qualified as an 'ausbrechender Gemeinschaftsakt' within the meaning of *Solange III*. Nevertheless, by the time the BVerfG was finally called upon by the Frankfurt Administrative court to disapply the banana regulation by qualifying it as 'ausbrechender Gemeinschaftsakt', the composition of the BVerfG had changed compared to the time of its *Solange III* ruling. Apparently, the BVerfG now found the time ripe to offer the ECJ a 'peace treaty' by essentially giving up the concept of 'ausbrechender Gemeinschaftsakt'.[296] As a result, in its *Solange IV* judgment the BVerfG held that it would review EC law measures only in the case that the minimum level of funda-

a way that is no longer covered by the German Act ratifying the EU Treaty, than the measures resulting therefrom would not be binding in Germany. The German organs would be prevented by reason of German Constitutional law from applying them. Accordingly, the BVerfG reviews whether the acts of European organs remain within the limits of the German ratification act or go beyond them. (author's own translation).

[294] For a detailed discussion see: Everling (1996); Lavranos (1999).

[295] See Lavranos (2005a).

[296] BVerfGE 102, 147 *Solange IV*. See generally: Pernice (2001); Grewe (2001).

mental rights protection was no longer guaranteed by EC organs on a general level.[297] Therefore, even though declaring an EC law measure an 'ausbrechender Gemeinschaftsakt' still remains possible, the conditions in place for this are extremely difficult to meet. In effect, only an act of the EC that goes completely against basic fundamental rights on a general level—and not only in one or several specific cases—would meet the criteria. The BVerfG thus moved back to its second *Solange* decision, thereby accepting the jurisdiction of the ECJ to a maximum extent, while at the same time limiting its own 'reserve jurisdiction' to a minimum.

The honeymoon, however, did not last very long. This is because the ECJ trespassed on another 'holy ground' of member state law, namely, criminal law. While member states had accepted that criminal law is an important and necessary component of the EU, as illustrated by its third pillar (Justice and Home Affairs, renamed Police and Justice Cooperation), the member states clearly did not intend to bring criminal law into the first pillar (the Community) and delegate competence to the EC to impose criminal law obligations with supranational force (that is, endowed with supremacy over the national laws of the member states). But the ECJ apparently thought otherwise and rendered groundbreaking judgments in *Pupino*[298] and *Commission v. Council*[299].

In *Pupino,* for the first time the ECJ stated that national courts must apply and interpret their national criminal procedural law as far as possible in accordance with the third pillar. In other words, a similar supremacy effect to that of the first pillar must be attached to the third pillar vis-à-vis national law.

In *Commission v. Council* the ECJ explicitly held for the first time that criminal law measures can be prescribed by the Community legislature for the purpose of maximum enforcement of EC law (in this case EC environmental law measures). This means that criminal law measures such as minimum and maximum fines and prison terms can be prescribed by EC law measures, i.e. first pillar measures.

Consequently, criminal law has entered the Community legal order and continues to expand.[300] When this development is combined with the continu-

---

[297] In its decision on the EC banana regulation BVerfGE 102, 147 *Solange IV*, the BVerfG defined the conditions as follows: Thus even after the decision in *Solange III*, requests by national courts before the BVerfG are inadmissible if they do not argue that the required level of fundamental rights protection within the EC, including ECJ case-law, has fallen below the standard as determined in *Solange II*. Accordingly, a request must prove in detail that a violation of fundamental rights by secondary EC law measures is general and that the level of protection has fallen below the minimum level as determined by the German Constitution. (author's own translation). The crucial condition is that a violation of fundamental rights by secondary EC law (such as the EC bananas regulation) must be specifically proven by showing that the absolute minimum level of fundamental rights is no longer generally guaranteed.

[298] Case C-105/03 *Pupino* [2005] ECR I-5285; see further: Spaventa (2007).

[299] Case C-176/03 *Commission v. Council* [2005] ECR I-7879; see also: Prinssen (2007).

[300] See eg: Case C-440/05 *Commission v. Council* [2007] ECR I-9097.

ous stream of far-reaching legislation in the third pillar, one may detect a forceful impact of EU law on national competencies in criminal law issues, which increasingly affects individuals directly.[301]

Therefore, when the BVerfG had the opportunity to decide on the German law implementing the European Arrest Warrant (EAW),[302] it is perhaps not surprising that it returned to the *Solange* formula as developed in its *Maastricht* judgment (*Solange III*). The *EAW* case concerned the issue of the constitutionality of the German act implementing the European Arrest Warrant, which was adopted within the third pillar as an EU Framework Decision. The crucial novelty of the EAW is the automatic binding force that is given to arrest orders from any EU member state and their automatic mutual recognition. In other words, a member state that is requested to arrest and transfer a citizen (including its own nationals) to another EU member state is no longer able to review that decision. The BVerfG, however, held that despite the current level of fundamental rights protection guaranteed by the ECJ, the ECHR and the other EU member states, the possibility of judicial review by the BVerfG in individual cases as guaranteed by the German Constitution could not be affected or excluded.[303] Accordingly, the 'reserve jurisdiction' of German courts, and ultimately of the BVerfG, in this matter remains intact.

In other words, the BVerfG continues to exercise its jurisdiction regarding third pillar measures irrespective of the existence of any (limited) ECJ jurisdiction in this area. Hence, in policy areas that inevitably affect fundamental rights in a substantial way, such as in matters of police and judicial cooperation (third pillar), the BVerfG is not yet prepared to limit its jurisdiction in the same way that it did regarding first pillar cases. Accordingly, one can now distinguish between a rather limited BVerfG 'reserve jurisdiction' in first pillar cases and a rather broad 'reserve jurisdiction' in third pillar cases.

In sum, it can be concluded that the *Solange* method has been used by the BVerfG in a flexible way in order to allow it to accommodate its jurisdictional relationship with the ECJ according to developments in ECJ case law, as well as developments on the more general European political scene. Accordingly, the *Solange* method enables the BVerfG to limit its jurisdiction in favour of ECJ jurisdiction depending on the current European level of fundamental rights protection. In short, a high level of fundamental rights protection means limited interference from the BVerfG, while a low level of fundamental rights protection means more interference from the BVerfG. Nevertheless, this flexibility should not be misunderstood as implying at any time a complete renunciation of jurisdiction, since the BVerfG has always maintained its 'reserve jurisdiction'.

---

301 See generally: Dowes / Lynskey (2008).

302 BVerfGE 113, 273 *Europäischer Haftbefehl*. See generally: Pollicino (2008); Schorkopf (2006).

303 *Ibid.*, para. 118.

2.4.2 The application of the *Solange* method at the international law level

Keeping the origins of the *Solange* method in mind, it is an interesting exercise to apply the method in those case studies in which it was not applied to discover what the effects of its application would have been. Thus, in this section the *Solange* method is tested hypothetically in all the case studies with the exception of the UNCLOS arbitral award in the *MOX plant* dispute and the *Bosphorus* judgment of the ECrtHR, since in those cases it was actually applied.

In the *MOX plant* dispute, instead of seizing its jurisdiction, the ECJ could have opted to decline its jurisdiction by applying the *Solange* method and referring the parties back to the UNCLOS arbitral tribunal for a final decision. In this way, the ECJ could have respected the existing jurisdiction of the UNCLOS Arbitral Tribunal and would have stopped the parties from re-litigating the dispute before the ECJ with the danger of potentially conflicting rulings. This would also have shortened the length of proceedings considerably.[304] Such a move by the ECJ would have been particularly risk-free in this case, since the UNCLOS Arbitral Tribunal showed so much consideration for the ECJ jurisdiction that it can be assumed that it would have shown similar consideration to the relevant ECJ jurisprudence. Thus, the risk of a possible divergent or conflict ruling would have been very low indeed. There was therefore no reason for the ECJ to be concerned about the uniform application of EC law within EC Member States. However, as discussed above, the ECJ did not show any sign that it would apply the *Solange* method towards the UNCLOS Arbitral Tribunal or any other international court/tribunal in general. Instead, it opted to claim maximum exclusive jurisdiction.

Similarly, neither the OSPAR Arbitral Tribunal was inclined to apply the *Solange* method. If it had, and consequently declined its jurisdiction, the parties would have had to go to the ECJ and relevant Community law would have been applied in the case. This in turn would have ensured the uniform application of EC law. At least the OSPAR Arbitral Tribunal was obliged when exercising its jurisdiction in this case to take relevant EC law and ECJ jurisprudence fully into account rather than adopting a divergent approach.

The application of the *Solange* method in the *IJzeren Rijn* dispute would have clearly made a huge difference to the outcome of the case. By applying the *Solange* method, the *IJzeren Rijn* Arbitral Tribunal would have declined its jurisdiction in favour of the ECJ. Since EC law was so obviously applicable in this case, this would have been the only appropriate solution. As a result, the ECJ would have been placed in a position to adjudicate the dispute, thereby ensuring

[304] It should be noted that even though the ECJ judgment in the *MOX Plant* dispute in which it seized jurisdiction regarding UNCLOS dates back to May 30, 2006, the UNCLOS arbitral tribunal terminated the proceeding only on June 6, 2008 without discussing the merits of the case. See UNCLOS Arbitral Tribunal, *MOX plant*, Order No. 6, Termination of Proceedings.

the proper and uniform application of EC law (especially the Habitats Directive) within EC Member States. Moreover, this would have prevented the *IJzeren Rijn* Arbitral Tribunal from formulating its inventive but flawed line of argument justifying its jurisdiction. Finally, it would have sent a strong message to EC Member States that they should stop trying to circumvent the ECJ when they think it is in their interest to do so. In this way, the authority of the ECJ would have been strengthened rather than weakened.

In the *Mexico soft drinks* case, the *Solange* method could have been applied by the WTO panel and Appellate Body in order to force the parties involved in the dispute to find a solution within the NAFTA dispute settlement body rather than litigate the same dispute again before another body.[305] As mentioned above, the *Mexico soft drinks* dispute is closely related to the much broader and long-standing sugar dispute between the US and Mexico. The WTO panel and Appellate Body had already found Mexico in breach of similar measures[306], so there was no need to re-litigate the dispute again before the WTO, in particular, since Mexico had apparently been trying for a long time to establish a NAFTA panel, but this was always blocked by the U.S.[307] If the establishment of a NAFTA panel could have been induced by applying the *Solange* method, it would also have strengthened the authority of the NAFTA dispute settlement system.

The *Brazilian Tyres* case is particularly interesting because it illustrates in one and the same dispute the consequences of both the application and non-application of the *Solange* method. On the one hand, the WTO panel applied the *Solange* method to the extent that it accepted that Brazil had adopted the disputed measure in order to implement the ruling of the MERCOSUR Arbitral Tribunal. Moreover, the WTO panel accepted the findings of the MERCOSUR Arbitral Tribunal as a fact of the case and did not review Brazil's defence strategy before that tribunal. In other words, even though the WTO panel exercised its jurisdiction in the case, it respected the jurisdiction of the MERCOSUR Arbitral Tribunal and took its award adequately into account by concluding that Brazil did not violate its WTO obligations when implementing the MERCOSUR Arbitral Tribunal decision. Thus, the WTO panel showed comity and delivered justice.

On the other hand, the WTO Appellate Body's approach towards the MERCOSUR Arbitral Tribunal's decision was quite the opposite. Although the WTO Appellate Body avoided reviewing the award of the MERCOSUR Arbitral Tribunal, it did discuss and censure the way Brazil implemented that award. Indeed, it went even further by criticizing Brazil's defence strategy and suggesting which provision Brazil ought to have relied upon before the MERCOSUR Arbitral Tribunal. In short, had the WTO Appellate Body applied the *Solange* method it could have ensured a more consistent resolution of the dispute and

---

305 NAFTA, *Review of the Final Determination of the Antidumping Investigation on Imports of High Fructose Corn Syrup, Originating from the United States of America*, Final Decision of 15.4.2002.

306 WTO Appellate Body Report, *Mexico – Corn Syrup*, WT/DS132/AB/RW of 22.10.2001.

307 See generally: Pauwelyn (2006).

would have ensured that the MERCOSUR and WTO law obligations remained congruent.

The ICJ's *Genocide Convention* judgment is another example illustrating that the application of the *Solange* method would have resulted in a different and – from the point of view of the uniformity of international law – preferable outcome. Even though the ICTY never challenged the jurisdiction of the ICJ and its competence to state the law regarding general international law issues, the ICJ considered it necessary to criticize the ICTY quite strongly and limit its jurisdiction. As a consequence thereof, divergent jurisprudences exist regarding the application of the proper test for determining whether or not the conditions for individual/state responsibility for international crimes are met. This creates unnecessary fragmentation concerning a vital point of general international law.

The ICJ could have avoided this situation if it had applied the *Solange* method. The ICJ could have easily adopted the approach of the ICTY, thereby ensuring the uniformity of international law and strengthening both the authority of the ICTY and its own. Moreover, and maybe even more importantly, the ICJ could have ensured that the horrific events in the Balkans be treated equally, i.e. that the perpetrators were actually punished.

To sum up, from the hypothetical application of the *Solange* method in these cases one can draw the following conclusions:

First, had the *Solange* method been applied by all courts and tribunals, the length of the proceedings would have been shortened and it would have resulted in a more consistent and uniform application of law.[308]

Second, the authority of the courts and tribunals would have been enhanced if they had applied the *Solange* method and thereby acted in a coordinated and efficient manner, which in turn would have strengthened the various dispute settlement systems involved. In other words, the consistent application of the *Solange* method would contribute towards a more rule-based dispute settlement culture between states.

Third, as a result of the previous points, true justice would have been delivered towards the parties, the courts and tribunals and the legal orders involved. In other words, the *Solange* method would have contributed to the rule of law.

In sum, it can be safely concluded that a systematic and consistent application of the *Solange* method by all courts and tribunals would allow for the adequate resolution of issues of jurisdictional competition. Nevertheless, the case studies also show that comity between the ECJ and other international courts and tribunals does not work by itself, but rather needs to be actively applied by all courts and tribunals.

[308] See extensively: Romano (2006).

CHAPTER 5

Conclusions

The previous Chapters have highlighted some of the fundamental issues of international law by examining the effects of the proliferation of international courts and tribunals.

States continue to set up international courts and tribunals in ever larger numbers essentially covering all fields of law. In principle, of course, this development must be welcomed as it allows states – and also other actors on the international plane – to resolve their disputes by peaceful means rather than through the use of arms. This institutionalization, or as some even argue constitutionalization, of international law adds to the multiplication of legal orders and (sub)regimes, and intensifies the interaction between them. Indeed, we are living in a multi-level, multi-polar, polycentric world that is dynamic, constantly changing and re-arranging the relationships between states, IOs, multinationals, NGOs, individuals etc.

The proliferation of international courts and tribunals, and with it their increasing power to shape these complex relationships, is just one aspect of the globalization and legalization of international relations. The main problem with this proliferation is the fact that it takes place in an uncoordinated fashion, without clearly formally regulating the jurisdictional relationship between all the various international courts and tribunals. This leads to competing or overlapping jurisdictions. As such, overlapping jurisdictions is neither a new problem nor does it have to be problematic *per se*. Indeed, there are many examples of multi-level judicial relations, within a federal state or between national courts and the ECJ, which function perfectly well. The difference, however, in international law level is the lack of hierarchical organization or any other form of coordination between the courts and tribunals to ensure that at the end of the process there will be one final and authoritative decision that resolves a dispute.

As a result of this uncoordinated proliferation of international courts and tribunals, the chance of conflicting jurisdiction significantly increases. This in turn can lead to a fragmentation of the international legal order, particularly if divergent or conflicting rulings on the same legal issues are rendered. Of course, using the metaphor of fragmentation presupposes that the international legal order was once a unified, well-organized legal order and is now threatened by the proliferation of international courts and tribunals. Obviously, that is a fiction, in the sense that the international legal order was never unified from the outset and probably never will be, but rather has developed over time in an uncoordinated manner. In other words, the uncoordinated development of international law is the normal state of affairs in international law. Therefore, occasional divergent or conflicting rulings by different international courts or tribunals are not regarded as problematic. However, what *is* regarded as problematic are major systemic inconsistencies that affect the legal orders or regimes concerned in their proper functioning, development and interaction with other legal orders or regimes. For instance, in the *MOX plant* case the ECJ's extensive claim of exclusive jurisdiction essentially prevents other designated dispute settlement bodies such as UNCLOS Arbitral Tribunals, ICJ or ITLOS from deciding disputes between EC Member States that may involve not only UNCLOS but also EC law provisions. Also, the fact that in the same dispute the OSPAR Arbitral Tribunal created conflicting rights and obligations as far as OSPAR and similar EC law provisions on access to information are concerned undermines the systemic co-functioning of EC and OSPAR provisions. Similarly, the outcome in the *Brazilian Tyres* dispute clearly impedes the authority of the MERCOSUR dispute settlement system by putting it under *de facto* review by the WTO Appellate Body.

Accordingly, the main aim of this study has been to search for a method or tool that would assist in providing systemic stability, consistency and harmony between all the various legal orders and regimes, thereby preserving trust in courts and tribunals, and thus ensure that justice is delivered.

It has become clear that, while the various hard-law options in theory promise to be effective tools for regulating jurisdictional competition, the unwillingness of states to implement them by amending the relevant legal instruments essentially eliminates their practical use.

Therefore, a solution depends on the judges and arbitrators, and their willingness to apply the soft-law tools discussed above. Besides the utilization of the *res judicata* and *lis pendens* principles, the general application of comity, in particular the *Solange* method, appears to be an effective tool for solving issues of jurisdictional competition in a system-preserving way.

However, the *Solange* method is only a 'voluntary restraint instrument', whose application depends solely on the attitude and readiness of each and every court and tribunal. Nonetheless, it is argued that the use of this method, and for that matter judicial comity in general, is part of the legal duty of each and every court to deliver justice. In doing so, taking due account of the existing jurisdiction of another court and subsequently coming to the decision to not exercise jurisdiction if the jurisdiction of another court is more appropriate is of course a task that all courts and tribunals should perform.[309]

Indeed, justice is part of the rule of law, which is the most fundamental principle that underpins the belief in supranational and international cooperation and its advantages for the individuals. Without firm rule of law at the supra- and international level, the shift in sovereignty that we currently perceive in so many different facets will bring few benefits for the individual.

However, even the application of the *Solange* method cannot avoid unsatisfying results in some cases. For example, the application of the *Solange* method effectively prevented Bosphorus from obtaining judicial review from the ECrtHR after the ECJ had rendered its judgment. Similarly, despite the application of comity by the UNCLOS Arbitral Tribunal, the inhabitants affected by the radioactive emissions of the MOX plant still do not have any independent answer as to the question of whether or not the UK violated its UNCLOS obligations.

---

[309] See generally on this point: Petersmann (2007a).

In contrast, the failure of the WTO Appellate Body to show more comity towards the MERCURSOR Arbitral Tribunal effectively means that Brazil remains a dumping site for used and retreaded tyres, which in turn will not help the country combat dengue. As a result, more dengue cases can be expected. Similarly, the failure to apply comity, or at least to make a sincere effort to bridge the gap between the different tests applied by the ICTY and ICJ, in the *Genocide Convention* case resulted in the inability of the ICJ to condemn the FRY, or rather Serbia, for the genocide it clearly had orchestrated. Evidently, such a judgment by the supreme UN court does no justice to the victims of these atrocities.

In sum, the challenge in each and every case is to find an appropriate balance between the interests of the parties to a dispute, the institutional and systemic interests of the courts and tribunals, the legal orders and regimes involved and the interests of the individuals concerned.

The general application of comity, in particular the *Solange* method can assist in finding this balance.

Bibliography

ADAM (2007)
S. Adam, 'Het Europees Hof van Justitie en andere internationale rechtsprekende organen: Enkele opmerkingen naar aanleiding van het MOX-Fabriek arrest' [2007] *Rev.B.D.I.* 113-147.

ALJAGHOUB (2006)
M. Aljaghoub, *The Advisory Function of the ICJ 1946-2005* (Berlin 2006).

ALVAREZ (2005)
J. E. Alvarez, *International Organizations as Law-makers* (Oxford 2005).

ALVAREZ (2003)
J.E. Alvarez, 'The new dispute settlers: (Half) Truths and Consequences' [2003] *Tex.Int'l L.J.* 405-444.

APPELTON / GRAF (2007)
A. Appleton / B. Graf, 'Freedom of Speech and Assembly versus Trade and Transit Rights: Roadblocks to EU and Mercosur Integration' [2007] *LIEI* 255-281.

BAUMÉ (2006)
T. Baumé, 'Competence of the Community to Conclude the New Lugano Convention on Jurisdiction and the Recognition and Enforcement of Judgements in Civil and Commercial Matters: Opinion 1/03 of 7 February 2006' [2006] *GLJ* 681-692 [available at: http://germanlawjournal.com/print.php?id=752].

BEN-EZER / BENDOR (2003)
A. Ben-Ezer / A. Bendor, 'The Constitution and Conflict-of-Laws Treaties: Upgrading the International Comity' [2003] *N.C.J.Int'l L.&C. Reg.* 1-34.

BENVENISTI / DOWNS (2007)
E. Benvenisti / G. Downs, 'The Empire's New Clothes: Political Economy and the Fragmentation of International Law' [2007] *Stan. L.Rev.* 595-631.

BRAZEL (2006)
P. Brazel, 'My neighbour doesn't like nuclear: Relationships between "nuclear" and "non-nuclear" countries' [2006] [available at: http://www.ecolo.org/documents/documents_in_english/Ireland-PETER-BRAZEL.doc].

BRÖHMER (2006)
J. Bröhmer, 'Die Bosphorus-Entscheidung des EGMR' [2006] *EuGRZ* 71-76.

BROWN (2007)
Chester Brown, *A Common Law of International Adjudication* (Oxford 2007).

BROWN / TRACHTMAN (2009)
Ch. Brown / J. Trachtman, 'Brazil – Measures affecting imports of retreaded tyres: A Balancing Act' [2009] *WT Rev.* 85-135.

BURGENTHAL (2001)
Th. Buergenthal, 'International Law and the proliferation of International Courts' [2001] *Bancaja Euromediterranean – Courses of International Law* 31-43.
BURKE-WHITE (2004)
W. Burke-White, 'International Legal Pluralism, Diversity or Cacophony?: New Sources of Norms in International Law – Symposium' [2004] *Mich. J. Intl'L.* 963-979.
CALLEWAERT (2008)
J. Callewaert, ''Unionisation' and 'Conventionisation' of fundamental rights in Europe: The interplay between Union and Convention law and its impact on the domestic legal systems of Union law' in: J. Wouters / A. Nollkaemper / E. de Wet, *The Europeanisation of International Law* (The Hague 2008) 109-135.
CANNIZZARO (2007)
E. Cannizzaro, 'Interconnecting International Jurisdictions: A contribution from the Genocide Decision of the ICJ' [2007/1] *EJLS* [available at: http://www.ejls.eu/1/5UK.htm].
CANOR (2000)
I. Canor, 'Primus inter Partes – Who is the ultimate guardian of fundamental rights in Europe?' [2000] *EL Rev.* 3-21.
CASS (2001)
D. Cass, 'The 'constitutionalization' of International Trade Law: Judicial Norm-Generation as the engine of constitutional development in International Trade' [2001] *EJIL* 39-75.
CASSESE (2007)
A. Cassese, 'The Nicaragua and Tadic tests revisited in light of the ICJ judgment on Genocide in Bosnia' [2007] *EJIL* 649-668.
CHALMERS (2006)
D. Chalmers et al., *EU Law* (Cambridge 2006).
CHARNEY (2002)
J. Charney, 'The 'horizontal' growth of International Courts and Tribunals: Challenges or Opportunities?' [2002] *ASIL Proc.* 369-380.
CHARNEY (1998)
J. Charney, 'Is International Law threatened by multiple International Tribunals?' [1998/271] *Recueil des Cours* 105-382.
CHESHIRE/NORTH/FAWCETT (2008)
G.C. Cheshire / P. North / J. Fawcett, *Private International Law* (Oxford 2008).
CHURCHILL / SCOTT (2004)
R. Churchill / J. Scott, 'The MOX Plant Litigation: The First Half-Life' [2004] *ICLQ* 643-676.

CHURCHILL / ULFSTEIN (2000)
R. Churchill / G. Ulfstein, 'Autonomous Institutional Arrangements in Multilateral Environmental Agreements: A little-noticed phenomenon in International Law' [2000] *AJIL* 623-659.

COGAN (2008)
J. Cogan, 'Competition and Control in International Adjudication' [2008] *Va. J. Int'l L.* 411-449.

COSTELLO (2006)
C. Costello, 'The Bosphorus ruling of the ECrtHR: Fundamental rights and blurred boundaries in Europe' [2006] *HRLRev.* 87-130.

CRAIG / DE BÚRCA (2008)
P. Craig / G. de Búrca, *EU Law* (Oxford 2008).

CRAIG (2002)
P. Craig, 'The ECJ, national courts and the supremacy of Community law' [2002]
[available at: http://www.ecln.net/rome2002/craig.pdf].

DASHWOOD (2000)
A. Dashwood, 'Preliminary rulings on the interpretation of mixed agreements' in: O'Keeffe (ed.), *Judicial Review in EU law – Liber Amicorum Lord Slynn of Hadley* (The Hague 2000) 167-175.

DAVEY (2006)
W. Davey, 'Dispute Settlement in the WTO and RTAs: A Comment' in L. Bartels /F. Ortino (eds.), *Regional Trade Agreements and the WTO Legal System* (Oxford 2006) 343-358.

DAVEY / SAPIR (2009)
W. Davey / A. Sapir, 'The Soft Drinks case: The WTO and Regional Agreements' [2009] *WT Rev.* 5-23.

DE ABREU FERREIRA (2008)
S. de Abreu Ferreira, 'Passive Access to Environmental Legislation in the EU – An Analysis of Recent Developments' [2008] *EEEL Rev.* 186-198.

DE WET (2006)
E. de Wet, 'The International Constitutional Order' [2006] *ICLQ* 51-76.

DIMITRIJEVIC / MILANOVIC (2008)
V. Dimitrijevic / M. Milanovic, 'The Strange Story of the Bosnian Genocide Case' [2008] *LJIL* 65-94.

DIPPEL (2004)
C. Dippel, *Die Kompetenzabgrenzung in der Rechtsprechung von EGMR und EuGH* (Berlin 2004).

DOUGLAS-SCOTT (2006A)
S. Douglas-Scott, 'A tale of two Courts: Luxembourg and Strasbourg and the growing European Human Rights aquis' [2006] *CML Rev.* 629-665.

DOUGLAS-SCOTT (2006B)
S. Douglas-Scott, 'Case-note on Bosphorus' [2006] *CML Rev.* 243-254.
DOWES / LYNSKEY (2008)
A. Dowes / O. Lynskey, 'The ever-longer arm of EC law: The extension of Community competence into the field of criminal law' [2008] *CML Rev.* 131-158.
DUPUY (2007A)
P.M. Dupuy, 'A doctrinal debate in the Globalisation Era: On the 'Fragmentation' of International Law' [2007/1] *EJLS* [available at: http://www.ejls.eu/1/4UK.pdf].
DUPUY (2007B)
P.M. Dupuy, 'The Unity of Application of International Law at the Global Level and the Responsibility of Judges' [2007/2] *EJLS* [available at: http://www.ejls.eu/index.php?mode=present&displayissue=2007-12].
DUPUY (1999)
P.M. Dupuy, 'The Danger of Fragmentation or Unification of the International Legal System and the ICJ' [1999] *NYU J. Int'l L.&Pol.* 791-807.
EECKHOUT (2007)
P. Eeckhout, 'Community Terrorism listings, Fundamental Rights and UN Security Council Resolutions – In Search of the Right Fit' [2007] *EConLRev.* 183-206.
EECKHOUT (2004)
P. Eeckhout, *EU External Relations* (Oxford 2004).
EVERLING (1996)
U. Everling, 'Will Europe slip on bananas? The banana judgment of the ECJ and national courts' [1996] *CML Rev.* 401-437.
FIGUEIREDO (2003)
L. Figueiredo, 'Dengue in Brazil: Past, Present and Future Perspective' [2003] *Dengue Bulletin* 25-33.
FOSTER HALABI (2005)
S. Foster Halabi, 'The Comity of Empagran: The Supreme Court decides that Foreign Competition Regulation limits American Antitrust Jurisdiction over international Cartels' [2005] *Harv. Int'l L.J.* 279-293.
FRANKLIN (2005)
Ch. Franklin, 'Flexibility vs. Legal Certainty: Article 307 EC and other issues in the aftermath of the Open Skies cases' [2005] *EFA Rev.* 79-115.
GAETA (2007)
P. Gaeta, 'On what conditions can a State be held responsible for Genocide?' [2007] *EJIL* 631-648.

GAMA SÁ CABRAL / LUCARELLI DE SALVIO (2008)
J. Gama Sá Cabral / G. Lucarelli de Salvio, 'Considerations on the Mercosur dispute settlement mechanism and the impact of its decisions in the WTO dispute settlement system' [2008] *JWT* 1013-1040.
GANTZ (2007)
D. A. Gantz, 'Settlement of Disputes under the Central America-Dominican Republic-United States Free Trade Agreement' [2007] *B.C.Int'l&Comp.L.Rev.* 331-410.
GAO / LIM (2008)
H. Gao / C. Lim, 'Saving the WTO from the risk of irrelevance: The WTO dispute settlement mechanism as a 'common good' for RTA disputes' [2008] *JIEL* 899-925.
GATTINI (2009)
A. Gattini, 'Case-note on Kadi' [2009] *CML Rev.* 213-239.
GATTINI (2007A)
A. Gattini, 'Breach of the obligation to prevent and reparation thereof in the ICJ's Genocide judgment' [2007] *EJIL* 695-713.
GATTINI (2007B)
A. Gattini, 'Evidentiary issues in the ICJ's Genocide judgment' [2007] *JICJ* 889-904.
GOLDSTONE / HAMILTON (2008)
R.J. Goldstone / R.J. Hamilton, 'Bosnia v. Serbia: Lessons from the Encounter of the International Court of Justice with the International Criminal Tribunal for the Former Yugoslavia' [2008] *LJIL* 95-112.
GONZALES (2004)
G. Gonzales, 'EC Fundamental Rights v. Human Rights in the case C-112/00 (Schmidberger)' [2004] *LIEI* 219-229.
GRAF VITZHUM (2008)
N. Graf Vitzhum, 'Les competence legislatives et jurisdictionelles del Communaute europeene dan la lutte contre le terrorisme – l'affaire Kadi' [2008] *ZEuS* 375-429.
GREWE (2001)
C. Grewe, 'Le 'traite de paix' avec la Cour de Luxembourg: L'arret de la Cour Constitutionnelle Allemande du 7.6.2000 Relatif au Reglement du Marche de la Banane' [2001] *Rev.trim.D.Eur.* 1-17.
GROOME (2008)
D. Groome, 'Adjudicating Genocide: Is the ICJ capable of judging state criminal responsibility?' [2008] *Fordham Int'l L.J.* 911-989.
GUILLAUME (2000)
G. Guillaume, 'Address to the UN General Assembly (delivered on 26.10.2000)'
[available at: http://www.icj-cij.org/court/index.php?pr=84&pt=3&p1=1&p2=3&p3=1].

GUILLAUME (1995)
G. Guillaume, 'The Future of International Judicial Institutions' [1995] *ICLQ* 848-862.
HAFNER (2004)
G. Hafner, 'Pros and Cons ensuing from Fragmentation of International Law, Diversity or Cacophony?: New Sources of Norms in International Law – Symposium' [2004] *Mich. J. Int'l L.* 849-863.
HAFNER (2000)
G. Hafner, 'Risks Ensuing from Fragmentation of International Law', Official Records of the General Assembly, 55th session, Supplement No. 10 (A/55/10), Annex [2000]
[available at: http://untreaty.un.org/ilc/reports/2000/repfra.htm].
HALBERSTAM / STEIN (2009)
D. Halberstam / E. Stein, 'The UN, the EU and the King of Sweden: Economic sanctions and individual rights in a plural world order' [2009] *CML Rev.* 13-72.
HARPAZ (2009A)
G. Harpaz, 'Judicial Review by the European Court of Justice of UN 'Smart Sanctions' Against Terror in the Kadi Dispute' [2009] *EFA Rev.* 65-88.
HARPAZ (2009B)
G. Harpaz, 'The ECJ and its relationships with the ECrtHR: The quest for enhanced reliance, coherence and legitimacy' [2009] *CML Rev.* 105-141.
HASSANIEN (2008)
M. Hassanien, 'Bilateralism and Multilateralism: Can Public International Law reconcile between them? Real options for further developments in WTO jurisprudence' [2008] *Asper Rev.Int'l B.&T.L.* 51-86.
HEER-REIßMANN (2006)
Ch. Heer-Reißmann, 'Straßburg oder Luxemburg? Der EGMR zum Grundrechtsschutz bei Verordnungen der EG in der Rechtssache Bosphorus' [2006] *NJW* 192-194.
HELFER (2008)
L. Helfer, 'Nonconsensual International Lawmaking' [2008] *Uni.Ill. L.Rev.* 71-125.
HELISKOSKI (2001)
J. Heliskoski, *Mixed agreements as a technique for organizing the international relations of the EC and its Member States* (The Hague 2001).
HENCKELS (2008)
C. Henckels, 'Overcoming jurisdictional isolationism at the WTO-FTA nexus: A potential approach for the WTO' [2008] *EJIL* 571-599.

HERRMANN (2002)
C. Herrmann, 'Common Commercial Policy after Nice: Sisyphus would have done a better job' [2002] *CML Rev.* 7-29.
HERZOG / GERKEN (2008)
R. Herzog / L. Gerken, 'Stop the ECJ' [2008] [available at http://www.cep.eu/fileadmin/user_upload/Pressemappe/CEP_in_den_Medien/Herzog-EuGH-Webseite_eng.pdf].
HEUN-REHN (2008)
S. Heun-Rehn, 'Kadi und Al Barakaat – Der EuGH, die Gemeinschaft und das Völkerrecht' [2008] *EL Rep.* 322-338.
HIRSCH (2005)
M. Hirsch, 'The Impact of the Advisory Opinion on Israel's Future Policy: International Relations Perspective' [2005] *J. Int'l L.&Int'l Rel.* 319-344.
HSU (2006)
L. Hsu, 'Applicability of WTO Law in Regional Trade Agreements: Identifying the Links' in L. Bartels / F. Ortino (eds.), *Regional Trade Agreements and the WTO Legal System* (Oxford 2006) 525-552.
JACKSON (2001)
J.H. Jackson, 'The WTO 'Constitution' and proposed reform: Seven Mantras Revisited' [2001] *JIEL* 67-78.
JACKSON (1999)
J.H. Jackson, 'Fragmentation or Unification among International Institutions: The World Trade Organization' [1999] *NYU J. Int'l L&Pol.* 823-831.
JACKSON (1998)
J.H. Jackson, *The World Trade Organization: Constitution and Jurisprudence* (London 1998).
JACKSON (1990)
J.H. Jackson, *Restructuring the GATT System* (New York 1990).
JACQUÉ (2005)
J.-P. Jacqué, 'Droit Communautaire et Convention européenne des droits de l'homme – L'arrêt Bosphorus, une jurisprudence 'Solange II' de la Cour européenne des droits de l'homme?' [2005] *Rev.trim.D.Eur.* 756-767.
JIMENEZ (2006)
A.A. Jimenez, 'The WTO Appellate Body Report on Mexico-Soft Drinks, and the Limits of the WTO Dispute Settlement System' [2006] *LIEI* 319-333.
KOMAREK (2005)
J. Komarek, 'Federal Elements in the Community Judicial System: Building Coherence in the Community Legal Order' [2005] *CML Rev.* 9-34.

KORNIS (2008)
M. Kornis, 'U.S. Corn Sweeteners and Mexican Sugar: Agreement at last!' [2008] *J. Int'l Comm.&Econ.* 51-62.
KOSKENNIEMI (2004)
M. Koskenniemi, 'Global Governance and Public International Law' [2004] *KJ* 241-254.
KOUTRAKOS (2006)
P. Koutrakos, *EU International Relations Law* (Oxford 2006).
KOUTRAKOS (2002)
P. Koutrakos, 'The interpretation of mixed-agreements under the preliminary ruling procedure' [2002] *EFA Rev.* 25-52.
KREß (2007)
C. Kreß, 'The International Court of Justice and the Elements of the Crime of Genocide' [2007] *EJIL* 619-629.
KUMM (2004)
M. Kumm, 'The Legitimacy of International Law: A Constitutionalist Framework of Analysis' [2004] *EJIL* 907-931.
KUNOY / DAWES (2009)
B. Kunoy / A. Dawes, 'Plate Tectonics in Luxembourg: The Ménage à Trois between EC law, International Law and the European Convention on Human Rights following the UN sanctions cases' [2009] *CML Rev.* 73-104.
LARIOS (2005)
P. Larios, 'The fight at the soda machine: Analysing the sweetener trade dispute between the US and Mexico before the WTO' [2005] *Am.U. Int'l L.Rev.* 649-702.
LAVRANOS (2009A)
N. Lavranos, 'Judicial Review of UN Sanctions by the ECJ' [2009] *NJIL* 343-359.
LARVANOS (2009B)
N. Lavranos, 'The epilogue in the MOX plant dispute: An end without findings' [2009] *EL Rep.* 117-121.
LAVRANOS (2009C)
N. Lavranos, 'Case note on Kadi' [2009] *LIEI* 157-183.
LARANOS (2008A)
N. Lavranos, 'In Dubio pro First Pillar: Recent developments in the delimitation of the competences of the EU and the EC' [2008] *EL Rep.* 311-319.
LAVRANOS (2008B)
N. Lavranos, 'The Solange-dialogue between the ECJ and the ECrtHR' [2008] *EL Rep.* 384-398.

LAVRANOS (2008C)
N. Lavranos, 'Towards a Solange method between international courts and tribunals?' in: T. Broude/Y. Shany (eds.), *The Shifting Allocation of Authority in International Law* (Oxford 2008) 217-235.
LAVRANOS / VIELLIARD (2008D)
N. Lavranos / N. Vielliard, 'Competing Jurisdictions between MERCOSUR and WTO' [2008] *L&PICT* 205-234.
LAVRANOS (2007)
N. Lavranos, 'The scope of the exclusive jurisdiction of the Court of Justice' [2007] *EL Rev.* 83-94.
LAVRANOS (2006A)
N. Lavranos, 'Case-note on Opinion 1/03 (Lugano Convention)' [2006] *CML Rev.* 1087-1100.
LAVRANOS (2006B)
N. Lavranos, 'Das So-lange-Prinzip im Verhältnis von EGMR und EuGH' [2006] *EuR* 79-92.
LAVRANOS (2006C)
N. Lavranos, 'Judicial Review of UN Sanctions by the CFI' [2006] *EFA Rev.* 471-490.
LAVRANOS (2006D)
N. Lavranos, 'Protecting its exclusive jurisdiction: The MOX plant judgment of the ECJ' [2006] *L&PICT* 479-493.
LAVRANOS (2006E)
N. Lavranos, 'The MOX plant and IJzeren Rijn disputes: Which court is the supreme arbiter?' [2006] *LJIL* 223-246.
LAVRANOS (2005A)
N. Lavranos, 'The Communitarization of WTO Dispute Settlement Reports: An Exception to the Rule of Law' [2005] *EFA Rev.* 313-338.
LAVRANOS (2005B)
N. Lavranos, 'Concurrence of Jurisdiction between the ECJ and other International Courts and Tribunals' [2005] *EEL Rev.* 213-225 and 240-251.
LAVRANOS (2004)
N. Lavranos, *Decisions of International Organizations in the European and Domestic legal orders of selected EU Member States* (Groningen 2004).
LAVRANOS (2003)
N. Lavranos, 'Case-note on open skies judgments' [2003] *LIEI* 81-91.
LAVRANOS (2002)
N. Lavranos, 'Multilateral Environmental Agreements: Who makes the binding decisions?' [2002] *EEL Rev.* 44-50.

LAVRANOS (1999)
N. Lavranos, 'Die Rechtswirkung von WTO panel reports im Europäischen Gemeinschaftsrecht sowie im deutschen Verfassungsrecht' [1999] *EuR* 289-308.

LEAL-ARCAS (2007)
R. Leal-Arcas, 'Choice of Jurisdiction in International Trade Disputes: Going Regional or Global?' [2007] *Minn. J. Int'l L.* 1-59.

LEATHLEY (2007)
Ch. Leathley, 'An Institutional Hierarchy to Combat the Fragmentation of International Law: Has the ILC Missed an Opportunity?' [2007] *NYU J. Int'l L.&Pol.* 259-299.

LINDNER (2007)
J. Lindner, 'Grundrechtsschutz in Europa: System einer Kollisionsdogmatik' [2007] *EuR* 160-193.

LINTON / KEBEDE TIBA (2009)
S. Linton / F. Kebede Tiba, 'The International Judge in an Age of Multiple International Courts and Tribunals' [2009] *Ch.J.Int'l L.* 407-470.

MALJEAN-DUBOIS (2008)
S. Maljean-Dubois, 'Le droit l'environnement comme exemple de la mondialisation des concepts juridiques: place et rôle des juridictions internationales et constitutionnelles', Final Report [2008] [available at : http://www.gip-recherche-justice.fr/IMG/pdf/170-RF_Maljean-Dubois_Droit_Environ.pdf].

MALJEAN-DUBOIS / MARTIN (2007)
S. Maljean-Dubois / J.-C. Martin, 'L'affaire de l'Usine MOX devant les tribunaux internationaux' [2007] *JDI* 437-471.

MALINTOPPI (2006)
L. Malintoppi, 'Methods of Dispute Resolution in Inter-State litigation: When States go to Arbitration rather than Adjudication' [2006] *L&PICT* 133-162.

MARTINEAU (2009)
A.-C. Martineau, 'The Rhetoric of Fragmentation: Fear and Faith in International Law' [2009] *LJIL* 1-28.

MARTINICO / FONTANELLI (2008)
G. Martinico / F. Fontanelli, 'The Hidden Dialogue: When Judicial Competitors Cooperate' [2008] *Gobal Jurist* [available at: http://www.bepress.com/cgi/viewcontent.cgi?article=1280&context=gj].

MARTINEZ (2003)
J. Martinez, 'Towards an International Judicial System' [2003] *Stan. L.Rev.* 429-529.

McDORMAN / CARON (2004)
T. McDorman / D. Caron, 'Access to Information under Article 9 OSPAR Convention' [2004] *AJIL* 331-341.

McLACHLAN / SHORE / WEINIGER (2007)
C. McLachlan / L. Shore / M. Weiniger, *International Investment Arbitration* (Oxford 2007).

MEYER (2006)
F. Meyer, 'The European Constitution and the Courts' in A. von Bogdandy / J. Bast, *Principles of European Constitutional Law* (Oxford 2006) 281-333.

MILANOVIC (2007)
M. Milanovic, 'State Responsibility for Genocide: A Follow-Up' [2007] *EJIL* 669-694.

MILLER (2002)
N. Miller, 'An International Jurisprudence? The Operation of 'Precedent' across International Tribunals' [2002] *LJIL* 483-526.

NATH (2007)
A. Nath, 'The Safta dispute settlement mechanism: An attempt to resolve or merely perpetuate conflict in the South Asian region?' [2007] *Am.U. Int'l L.Rev* 333-358.

OEN (2005)
R. Oen, *Internationale Streitbeilegung im Kontext gemischter Verträge der EG und ihrer Mitgliedstaaten* (Berlin 2005).

ORREGO VICUÑA (2004)
F. Orrego Vicuña, *International Dispute Settlement in an Evolving Global Society* (Cambridge 2004).

PAULUS (2004)
A. Paulus, 'From Neglect to Defiance: The US and International Adjudication' [2004] *EJIL* 783-812.

PAUWELYN (2007)
J. Pauwelyn, 'Legal Avenues to 'Multilaterlizing Regionalism': Beyond Article XXIV' [2007]
[available at: http://www.wto.org/english/tratop_e/region_e/con_sep07_e/pauwelyn_e.pdf].

PAUWELYN (2006)
J. Pauwelyn, 'Adding Sweeteners to Softwood Lumber: the WTO-NAFTA 'Spaghetti Bowl' is Cooking' [2006] *JIEL* 197-206.

PAUWELYN (2004)
J. Pauwelyn, 'Going Global, Regional, or Both? Dispute Settlement in the Southern African Development Community (SADC) and overlaps with the WTO and other jurisdictions' [2004] *Minn. J.Gl.T.* 231-304.

PAVON / SCHMIDT (2007)
D. Pavon / J.P. Schmidt, 'In the Footsteps of the ECJ: First Decision of the Permanent Mercosur-Tribunal' [2007] *LIEI* 283-293.

PELLET (2004)
A. Pellet, 'Strengthening the Role of the International Court of Justice as the principle judicial organ of the UN' [2004] *L&PICT* 159-180.
PEREZ (1998)
A. Perez, 'WTO and UN Law: Institutional Comity in National Security' [1998] *Yale J. Int'l L.* 301-379.
PERNICE (2001)
I. Pernice, 'Les bananes et les droits fondamentaux: La Cour Constitutionnelle Allemande fait le point' [2001] *CDE* 427-440.
PETERS (2006)
A. Peters, 'Compensatory Constitutionalism: The Function and Potential of Fundamental International Norms and Structures' [2006] *LJIL* 579-610.
PETERSMANN (2008)
E.-U. Petersmann, 'Human Rights, International Economic Law and 'Constitutional' Justice' [2008] *EJIL* 769-798.
PETERSMANN (2007A)
E.-U. Petersmann, 'Multilevel Judicial Governance of International Trade requires a Common conception of Rule of Law and Justice' [2007] *JIEL* 529-551.
PETERSMANN (2007B)
E.-U. Petersmann, 'Do Judges Meet Their Constitutional Obligation to Settle Disputes in Conformity with Principles of Justice and International Law?' [2007/2] *EJLS*
[available at: http://www.ejls.eu/2/22UK.htm].
PISCTIELLO / SCHMIDT (2007)
D. Pisctiello / J. Schmidt, 'In the Footsteps of the ECJ: First Decision of the Permanent MERCOSUR-Tribunal' [2007] *LIEI* 283-293.
POLLICINO (2008)
O. Pollicino, 'European Arrest Warrant and Constitutional Principles of the Member States: a Case Law-Based Outline in the Attempt to Strike the Right Balance between Interacting Legal Systems' [2008] *GLJ* 1313-1355.
[available at: http://www.germanlawjournal.com/pdf/Vol09No10/PDF_Vol_09_No_10_1313-1354_Developments_Pollicino.pdf].
PRINSSEN (2007)
J. Prinssen, 'Doctrinal Legal Effects of EU criminal law: A transfer of EC law doctrines?' in N. Lavranos / D. Obradovic (eds.), *Interface between EU Law and National Law* (Groningen 2007) 313-331.
RAJKOVIC (2008)
N. Rajkovic, 'On 'Bad Law' and 'Good Politics': The Politics of the ICJ Genocide case and its interpretation' [2008] *LJIL* 885-910.

RAMSEY (1998)
M. Ramsey, 'Escaping International Comity' [1998] *Iowa L. Rev.* 893-952.

RAO (2004)
P.S. Rao, 'Multiple International Judicial Forums: A Reflection of the Growing Strength of International Law or its Fragmentation, Diversity or Cacophony?: New Judicial Sources of Norms in International Law – Symposium' [2004] *Mich. J. Int'l L.* 929-961.

REINISCH (2004)
A. Reinisch, 'The Use and Limits of Res Judicata and Lis Pendens' [2004] *L&PICT* 37-77.

RÖBEN (2000)
V. Röben, 'Institutional developments under modern environmental agreements' [2000] *MPYbUN L.* 363-443.

ROMANO (2007)
C. Romano, 'Case-note on MOX plant' [2007] *AJIL* 171-179.

ROMANO (2006)
C. Romano, 'From the Consensual to the Compulsory Paradigm in International Adjudication: Elements for a Theory of Consent' [2006] *NYU School of Law* 2006, Paper 20, [available at: http://lsr.nellco.org/nyu_plltwp/20/].

ROMANO (1999)
C. Romano, 'The Proliferation of International Judicial Bodies: The Pieces of the Puzzle' [1999] *NYU J. Int'l L.&Pol.* 709-751.

SAUER (2008)
H. Sauer, *Jurisdiktionskonflikte in Mehrebenensystemen: Die Entwicklung eines Modells zur Lösung von Konflikten zwischen Gerichten unterschiedlicher Ebenen in vernetzten Rechtsordnungen* (Berlin/ Heidelberg 2008).

SCHORKOPF (2006)
F. Schorkopf, *Der Europäische Haftbefehl vor dem Bundesverfassungsgericht* (Tübingen 2006).

SCHWEBEL (1999)
S. M. Schwebel, 'Address to the Plenary Session of the UN General Assembly (delivered on 26.10.1999) [available at: http://www.icj-cij.org/court/index.php?pr=87&pt=3&p1=1&p2=3&p3=1].

SHAHABUDEEN (2002)
M. Shahabuddeen, 'Consistency in holdings of International Tribunals' in: N. Ando / E. McWhinney / R. Wolfrum (eds.) *Liber Amicorum Judge Shigeru Oda* (The Hague 2002) 633-650.

SHANY (2007)
Y. Shany, *Regulating Jurisdictional Relations between national and international courts* (Oxford 2007).

SHANY (2004)
Y. Shany, 'The First MOX plant Award: The need to harmonize competing environmental regimes and dispute settlement procedures' [2004] *LJIL* 815-828.
SHANY (2003)
Y. Shany, *The Competing jurisdiction of International courts and tribunals* (Oxford 2003).
SHAW (2008)
M. Shaw, *International Law* (Cambridge 2008).
SIMMA (2004)
B. Simma, 'Fragmentation in a positive light, Diversity or Cacophony?: New Sources of Norms of International Law – Symposium' [2004] *Mich. J. Int'l L.* 845-848.
SLAUGHTER (2004)
A.-M. Slaughter, *A New World Order* (Princeton 2004).
SLAUGHTER (2003)
A.M. Slaughter, 'A Global Community of Courts' [2003] *Harv. Int'l L. J.* 191-219.
SLAUGHTER (2000)
A.M. Slaugter, 'Judicial Globalization' [2000] *Va. J. Int'l L.* 1103-1124.
SÖDERLUND (2005)
Ch. Söderlund, 'Lis Pendes, Res Judicata and the issue of parallel judicial proceedings' [2005] *J. Int'l Arb.* 301-322.
SPAVENTA (2007)
E. Spaventa, 'Opening Pandora's Box: Some Reflections on the Constitutional Effects of the Decision in Pupino' [2007] *EConLRev.* 5-24.
SPELLISCY (2001)
S. Spelliscy, 'The Proliferation of International Tribunals: A chink in the armor' [2001] *Col. J. Transnat'l. L.* 143-175.
SPIELMANN (1999)
D. Spielmann, 'Human Rights case law in the Strasbourg and Luxembourg courts: Conflicts, Inconsistencies and Complementarities' in: P. Alston (ed.), *The EU and Human Rights* (Oxford 1999) 757-780.
STEINER (2006)
J. Steiner, et al., *EU Law* (Oxford 2006).
SUGIHARA (2002)
T. Sugihara, 'The ICJ – Towards a higher role in the International Community' in: N. Ando et al. (eds.), *Liber Amicorum Judge Shigeru Oda* (The Hague 2002) 227-235.
TAN (2005)
D. Tan, 'Anti-suit Injunctions and the vexing problem of Comity' [2005] *Va. J. Int'l L.* 283-356.

TINY (2005)
N. Tiny, 'Regionalism and the WTO: Mutual Accommodation at the Global Trading System' [2005] *Int'l T.L.&Reg.* 126-145.
TRIDIMAS (2009)
T. Tridimas, 'Terrorism and the ECJ: The Empowerment and democracy in the EC legal order' [2009] *EL Rev.* 103-126.
TRIDIMAS / GUITIERREZ-FONS (2009)
T. Tridimas / J. Guitierrez-Fons, 'EU law, International law and economic sanctions against terrorism: The Judiciary in distress?' [2009] *Fordham Int'l L. J.* 660-730.
VACEK-ARANDA (2006)
A. Vacek-Aranda, 'Sugar wars: dispute settlement under NAFTA and the WTO as seen through the lens of the HFCS case and its effects on US-Mexican relations' [2006] *Tex.Hisp. J.L.&Pol.* 121-160.
VAN BLADEL (2005)
I. van Bladel, 'The Iron Rhine Arbitration Case: On the Right Legal Track? An analysis of the award and of its relation to the Law of the European Community' [2005] *HYbIL* 3-22.
VAN CALSTER (2008)
G. van Calster, 'Faites Vos Jeux – Regulatory Autonomy and the World Trade Organisation after Brazil Tyres' [2008] *JEL* 121-136.
VAN CALSTER (2007)
G. van Calster, 'The WTO Panel Report on Brazil Tyres – Advanced Waste Management Theory Entering the Organisation?' [2007] *EEL Rev.* 304-308.
VAN DAMME (2006)
I. van Damme, 'What Role is there for Regional International Law in the Interpretation of the WTO Agreements?' in L. Bartels / F. Ortino (eds.), *Regional Trade Agreements and the WTO Legal System* (Oxford 2006) 553-576.
VINUESA (2006)
R. Vinuesa, 'The MERCOSUR settlement of disputes system' [2006] *L&PICT* 77-87.
VON BOGDANDY (2004)
A. von Bogdandy, 'Globalization and Europe: How to Square Democracy, Globalization and International Law' [2004] *EJIL* 885-906.
VRANES (2009)
E. Vranes, 'Gemischte Abkommen und die Zuständigkeit des EuGH – Grundfragen und neuere Entwicklungen in den Außenbeziehungen' [2009] *EuR* 44-79.

WARBRICK (2005)
C. Warbrick, 'The 'Iron Rhine' ('IJzeren Rijn') arbitration: its contribution to international law' in *The Iron Rhine Arbitration Award 2005* (The Hague 2007) 153-193.
WEILER (1996)
J.H.H. Weiler, 'The Jurisprudence of Human Rights in The European Union, Integration and Disintegration, Values and Processes' [1996] *Jean Monnet Working Paper* 2/96
[available at: http://www.jeanmonnetprogram.org/papers/96/9602.html].
WENNERÅS (2008)
P. Wennerås, 'Towards an ever greener Union? Competence in the field of the environment and beyond' [2008] *CML Rev.* 1645-1685.
YOUNG (2005)
A. Young, 'The Charter, Constitution and Human Rights: is this the beginning or the end for human rights protections by Community law?' [2005] *EPL* 219-240.

Table of Cases

Judgments and Opinions of the European Court of Justice and Opinions of Advocate Generals

Case 22/70 *AETR* [1971] ECR 263
Case 21-24/72 *International Fruit Company* [1972] ECR 1219
Case 4/73 *Nold* [1974] ECR 491
Case 44/79 *Hauer* [1979] ECR 3727
Case 283/81 *CILFIT* [1982] ECR 3415
Case 104/81 *Kupferberg* [1982] ECR 3641
Case 5/88 *Wachauf* [1989] ECR 2609
Case C-260/89 *ERT* [1991] ECR I-2925
ECJ Opinion 1/91 *EEA* [1991] ECR I-6079
ECJ Opinion 1/94 *WTO Agreement* [1994] ECR I-5267
ECJ Opinion 2/94 *Accession to the ECHR* [1996] ECR I-1759
Case C-84/95 *Bosphorus* [1996] ECR I-3953
Case C-61/94 *Commission* v. *Germany* [1996] ECR I-3989
Case C-321/96 *WilhelmMecklenburg* v. *Kreis Pinneberg – Der Landrat* [1998] ECR I-3809
Case C-217/97 *Commission* v. *Germany* [1999] ECR I-5087
Case C-60/00 *Carpenter* [2002] ECR I-6279
Case C-413/99 *Baumbast* [2002] ECR I-7091
Case C-112/00 *Schmidberger* [2003] ECR I-5659
Case C-316/01 *Glawischnig* [2003] ECR I-5995
Case C-233/00 *Commission* v. *France* [2003] ECR I-6625
Case C-224/01 *Köbler* [2003] ECR I-10239
Case C-117/01 *K.B.* [2004] ECR I-541
Case C-453/00 *Kühne & Heitz* [2004] ECR I-837
Case C-200/02 *Chen* [2004] ECR I-9925
Case C-125/04 *Denuit and Cordenier* v. *Transorient* [2005] ECR I-923
Case C-186/04 *Housieaux* [2005] ECR I-3299
Case C-105/03 *Pupino* [2005] ECR I-5285
Case C-176/03 *Commission* v. *Council* [2005] ECR I-7879
Case C-6/04 *Commission* v. *UK* [2005] ECR I-9017
Opinion of AG Colomer in Case C-461/03 *Gaston Schul* [2005] ECR I-10513
Case C-461/03 *Gaston Schul* [2005] ECR I-10513
ECJ Opinion 1/03 *Lugano Convention* [2006] ECR I-1145
Opinion of AG Maduro in Case C-459/03 *Commission* v. *Ireland* [2006] ECR I-4635
Case C-459/03 *Commission* v. *Ireland* [2006] ECR I-4635
Case C-239/04 *Commission* v. *Portugal* [2006] ECR I-10183
Case C-508/04 *Commission* v. *Austria* [2007] ECR I-3787
Case C-388/05 *Commission* v. *Italy* [2007] ECR I-7555
Case C-440/05 *Commission* v. *Council* [2007] ECR I-9097
Case C-418/04 *Commission* v. *Ireland* [2007] ECR I-10947
Opinion of AG Kokott in Case C-308/06 *Intertanko* [2008] ECR I-4057

Case C-308/06 *Intertanko* [2008] ECR I-4057
Case C-188/07 *Commune de Mesquer* [2008] ECR I-4501
Joined Cases C-402/05 P and C-415/05 P *Kadi* and *Al Barakaat International Foundation* judgment of 3.9.2008
[all available at: http://curia.europa.eu/jurisp/cgi-bin/form.pl?lang=en]

Judgments of the Court of First Instance

Case T-315/01 *Kadi* [2005] ECR II-3649
[available at: http://curia.europa.eu/jurisp/cgi-bin/form.pl?lang=en]

Judgments of the European Court of Human Rights

Case of *Cantoni* v. *France*, judgment of 15.11.1996
Case of *Matthews* v. *UK*, judgment of 18.2.1999
Case of *Bosphorus* v. *Ireland*, decision on admissibility of 13.9.2001
Case of *Bosphorus* v. *Ireland*, judgment of 30.6.2005
[all available at: http://www.echr.coe.int/ECHR/EN/Header/Case-Law/HUDOC/HUDOC+database/]

WTO Panel and Appellate Body reports

WT/DS2/AB/R, *US – Standards for Reformulated and Conventional Gasoline* (Appellate Body report of 20.5.1996)
WT/DS33/AB/R, *US – Wool Shirts and Blouses* (Appellate Body report of 23.5.1997)
WT/DS50/AB/R, *India – Patents (U.S.)* (Appellate Body report of 19.12.1997)
WT/DS48/AB/R, *EC – Hormones* (Appellate Body report of 16.1.1998)
WT/DS18/AB/R, *Australia – Measures affecting importation of Salmon* (Appellate Body report of 20.10.1998)
WT/DS34/R, *Turkey – Restrictions on Imports of Textile and Clothing Products* (Panel report of 31.5.1999)
WT/DS34/AB/R, *Turkey – Restrictions on Imports of Textile and Clothing Products* (Appellate Body report of 22.10.1999)
WT/DS136/AB/R, WT/DS162/AB/R, *US – Anti-Dumping Act of 1916* (Appellate Body report of 28.8.2000)
WT/DS132/AB/RW, *Mexico – Corn Syrup* (Appellate Body report of 22.10.2001)
WT/DS108/AB/RW, *US – FSC* (Appellate Body report of 14.1.2002)
WT/DS308/R, *Mexico-Tax measures on soft drinks and other beverages* (Panel report of 7.10. 2005)
WT/DS308/AB/R, *Mexico – Tax measures on soft drinks and other beverages* (Appellate Body report of 6.3.2006)
WT/DS308/15, *Mexico – Tax measures on soft drinks and other beverages* (Agreement under Article 21.3(b) DSU of 5.7.2006)
WT/DS308/16, *Mexico – Tax measures on soft drinks and other beverages* (Status Report by Mexico of 12.1.2007)

WT/DS332/R, *Brazil – Measures Affecting Imports of Retreaded Tyres* (Panel report of 12.6.2007)
WT/DS332/AB/R, *Brazil – Measures Affecting Imports of Retreaded Tyres* (Appellate Body report of 3.12.2007)
WT/DS332/16, *Brazil – Measures Affecting Imports of Retreaded Tyres* (Award of the Arbitrator of 29.8.2008)
[all available at: http://www.wto.org/english/tratop_e/dispu_e/dispu_status_e.htm]

International Court of Justice
Nicaragua v. *US*, judgment of 27.6.1986
Genocide Convention – Bosnia-Herzegovina v. *Serbia and Montenegro*, judgment of 26.2.2007
Genocide Convention – Bosnia-Herzegovina v. *Serbia and Montenegro*, Dissenting Opinion of Vice President Al-Khasawneh of 18.10.2007
[all available at: www.icj-cij.org/]

International Criminal Tribunal for the Former Yugoslavia
Appeals Chamber, *Tadic*, judgment of 15.7.1999
Appeals Chamber, *Aleksovski*, judgment of 24.3.2000
Appeals Chamber, *Prosecutor* v. *Zejnil Delalic, Zdravko Mucic (aka 'Pavo'), Hazim Delic and Esad Landzo (aka 'Zenga')*, judgment of 20.2.2001
[all available at: http://www.icty.org/action/cases/4]

International Tribunal of the Law of the Sea
MOX plant, Request for Provisional Measures, Order of 3.12.2001
[available at: www.itlos.org]

International Arbitral Tribunals
UNCLOS Arbitral Tribunal, *MOX plant*, Suspension of Proceedings on Jurisdiction and Merits and Request for further Provisional Measures, Order No. 3 of 24.6.2003
OSPAR Arbitral Tribunal, *MOX plant*, Final Award of 2.7.2003
Ad hoc Arbitral Tribunal, *IJzeren Rijn*, Arbitral Award of 24.5.2005
UNCLOS Arbitral Tribunal, *MOX plant*, Order No. 6, Termination of proceedings, 6.6.2008
[all available at: http://www.pca-cpa.org/]

NAFTA
Review of the Final Determination of the Antidumping Investigation on Imports of High Fructose Corn Syrup, Originating from the US, Final Decision of 15.4.2002
[available at http://registry.nafta-sec-alena.org/cmdocuments/2b2bod9a-570f-4f8c-bd47-a66bf4553ba2.pdf]

MERCOSUR

Ad hoc Arbitral Tribunal, *Uruguay* v. *Brazil (Remoulded Tyres)*, 9.1.2002
[available at: http://www.mercosur.int/msweb/portal%20intermediario/pt/controversias/VI%20LAUDO.pdf]
Ad hoc Arbitral Tribunal, *Uruguay* v. *Argentina – Import prohibition of remoulded tyres from Uruguay*, 25.10.2005
[available at: http://www.sice.oas.org/Dispute/mercosur/laudo%20neumaticos_005_s.pdf]
Permanent Review Court, *Uruguay* v. *Argentina – Import prohibition of remoulded tyres from Uruguay*, 22.12.2005
[available at: http://www.mercosur.int/msweb/SM/es/Controversias/TPR/TPR_Laudo001-2005_Importacion%20de%20Neumaticos%20Remoldeados.pdf]

Germany

BVerfGE 37, 327, *Solange I*, 29.5.1974
BVerfGE 73, 339, *Solange II*, 22.10.1986
BVerfGE 89, 155, *Solange III*, 12.10.1993
BVerfGE 102, 147, *Solange IV*, 7.6.2000
BVerfGE 113, 273, *Europäischer Haftbefehl*, 18.7.2005
[all available at: http://www.servat.unibe.ch/dfr/dfr_bvbd100.html]

United States of America

Supreme Court, *Hilton* v. *Guyot*, 159 U.S. 113, 163-64 (1895)
Supreme Court, *Intel Corp.* v. *Advanced Micro Devices*, 542 U.S. 241 (2004)
[all available at: http://supreme.justia.com/index.html]